A
GAZETTEER OF
MARYLAND
AND
DELAWARE

By
HENRY GANNETT

Two Volumes in One

CLEARFIELD COMPANY

Reprinted for
Clearfield Company, Inc. by
Genealogical Publishing Co., Inc.
Baltimore, Maryland
1994

Originally published: Washington, D.C., 1904
as *A Gazetteer of Maryland,*
U.S. Geological Survey, Bulletin No. 231
and *A Gazetteer of Delaware,*
U.S. Geological Survey, Bulletin No. 230
Reprinted: Two volumes in one
Genealogical Publishing Co., Inc.
Baltimore, 1976, 1979
A Gazetteer of Maryland is reprinted from a volume in
the George Peabody Department, Enoch Pratt Free Library
Baltimore, Maryland
A Gazetteer of Delaware is reprinted from a volume in
the Eleutherian Mills Historical Library
Wilmington, Delaware
Library of Congress Catalogue Card Number 75-37016
International Standard Book Number 0-8063-0703-X
Made in the United States of America

Bulletin No. 231

Series F, Geography, 39

DEPARTMENT OF THE INTERIOR

UNITED STATES GEOLOGICAL SURVEY

CHARLES D. WALCOTT, DIRECTOR

A

GAZETTEER OF MARYLAND

BY

HENRY GANNETT

WASHINGTON
GOVERNMENT PRINTING OFFICE
1904

LETTER OF TRANSMITTAL.

DEPARTMENT OF THE INTERIOR,
UNITED STATES GEOLOGICAL SURVEY,
Washington, D. C., March 9, 1904.

SIR: I have the honor to transmit herewith, for publication as a bulletin, a gazetteer of Maryland.

Very respectfully,   HENRY GANNETT,
                                                Geographer.

Hon. CHARLES D. WALCOTT,
    Director United States Geological Survey.

3

A GAZETTEER OF MARYLAND.

By Henry Gannett.

GENERAL DESCRIPTION OF THE STATE.

Maryland is one of the Eastern States, bordering on the Atlantic Ocean, about midway between the northern and southern boundaries of the country. It lies between latitudes 37° 53' and 39° 44', and between longitudes 75° 04 and 79° 33'. Its neighbors are Pennsylvania on the north, West Virginia and Virginia on the west and south, and Delaware on the east. Its north boundary is Mason and Dixon's line, and its east boundary is, in part, a nearly north-south line separating it from Delaware and Pennsylvania, and, in part, the Atlantic Ocean. On the south the boundary is an irregular line across the peninsula separating Chesapeake Bay from the Atlantic Ocean; then across Chesapeake Bay to the southern point of the entrance to Potomac River; thence following the low-water line on the south bank of the Potomac to the head of the north branch of that river, at a point known as Fairfax Stone, excepting the area of the District of Columbia. The west boundary is a meridian drawn through Fairfax Stone northward to Mason and Dixon's line.

The gross area of the State, including that part of Chesapeake Bay in its borders, the broad estuaries at the mouths of the rivers, and the lagoons on the Atlantic coast, is 12,210 square miles, of which 9,860 square miles are land area

The topography of the State is extremely varied, ranging from level lands, but slightly elevated above the sea, to mountains and plateaus in the western part of the State, 3,000 feet in altitude. The peninsula east of Chesapeake Bay and a narrow strip west of that body of water constitute what is known as the Coastal Plain. This has an area of 5,000 square miles, or more than one-half of the land area of the State. The peninsula is very low and level, nowhere rising 100 feet above tide, and much of it, especially near the shore of the Atlantic Ocean and Chesapeake Bay, is marshy. The Atlantic coast is bordered by sand bars, including broad lagoons of shallow water on their landward side. On the west side of Chesapeake Bay the Coastal Plain reaches an altitude of 300 feet in places, and shows much relief. Of the twenty-three counties of the State, the following are comprised in the Coastal Plain: Worcester, Somerset, Wicomico, Dorchester, Caroline, Talbot, Queen Anne, Kent, and Cecil, on the peninsula, and Prince George, Charles, Calvert, St. Mary, and Anne Arundel west of Chesapeake Bay.

Along a line running through Havre de Grace, Baltimore, and Washington the granitic rocks rise to the surface. This is called the "fall line," from the fact that streams have rapids or falls where they flow across the first hard ledges. West of this line granite or allied rocks predominate, while east of it, on the Coastal Plain, are soft Cretaceous and Tertiary formations. This region extends from the fall line to the Blue Ridge and has an area of about 2,500 square miles. It is known as the Piedmont Plateau and comprises the following counties: Montgomery, Howard, Baltimore, Harford, Carroll, and Frederick. This region presents much more relief and is higher than the Coastal Plain.

The third zone, that of the Appalachian Mountains, extends from the Blue Ridge to the west boundary of the State, and has an area of about 2,000 square miles. It includes the counties of Washington, Allegany, and Garrett. In the main this region consists of an alternation of valleys and mountain ridges, the latter rising to altitudes of 2,000 and 3,000 feet. In the western part, mainly in Garrett County, is a plateau with a rolling surface 2,500 feet above sea level.

The mean elevation of the State is estimated at 350 feet. The areas in different zones of altitude are as follows:

Elevations in Maryland.

	Square miles.
Sea level to 100 feet	7,400
100 to 500 feet	2,000
500 to 1,000 feet	1,700
1,000 to 1,500 feet	300
1,500 to 2,000 feet	410
2,000 to 3,000 feet	400

Maryland was first settled in 1634 under a charter to Lord Baltimore, settlement being made at St. Marys. It was one of the thirteen original States, having adopted the Constitution on April 28, 1788. In 1791 the State ceded to the General Government for the purposes of a capital an area of about 70 square miles, which constitutes the present District of Columbia. The following table shows the growth of population in the State from the first census in 1790 to the latest in 1900:

Population of Maryland at each census since 1790.

Census.	Population.	Increase.
		Per cent.
1790	319,723	....
1800	341,548	6.8
1810	380,546	11.4
1820	407,350	7.0
1830	447,040	9.7
1840	470,019	5.1
1850	583,034	24.0
1860	687,049	17.8
1870	780,894	13.7
1880	934,943	19.7
1890	1,042,390	11.5
1900	1,188,044	14.0

In 1730 Maryland was the sixth State in the Union in population.
In 1900, although its inhabitants were 3.7 times as numerous, it had
dropped to the twenty-sixth in rank, owing to the rapid growth of the
newer States in the Mississippi Valley. In 1900 the average density
of population was 120 persons to the square mile. It has five cities
which exceed 6,000 inhabitants, of which Baltimore has over half a
million. The other four are as follows: Cumberland, 17,128; Hagerstown, 13,591; Frederick, 9,296; and Annapolis, the capital, 8,525.
These five cities contain 46.9 per cent of the population of the entire
State. In cities of more than 2,500 inhabitants live 48.8 per cent,
or nearly one-half the population of the State, while the remainder,
51.2 per cent, may be regarded as rural. In 1900 the population was
divided almost equally between the two sexes, 49.6 per cent being
males and 50.4 per cent being females. The negro population, though
large for a border State, is diminishing in proportion to the whites.
In 1900 the whites formed 80.2 per cent and the negroes 19.8 per cent,
or nearly one-fifth of the population. The number of foreign-born
inhabitants was also small, the persons of native birth forming 92.1
per cent, while those born in foreign countries were 7.9 per cent.
Immigration from other States has not been large, since it is found
that of the native population 13 per cent were born in other States.

For a State containing so large a proportion of negroes, the illiteracy
is slight. In 1900, persons of 10 years of age and upward who were
unable to read and write constituted 11.1 per cent of the population.
The illiterates comprised only 4.1 per cent of the native whites over
10 years old, 13.4 per cent of the foreign born, and 35.1 per cent of
the negroes.

Of the population, 15 years old and upward, 37.9 per cent were single; 52.9 per cent married; 8.5 per cent widowed; 0.2 per cent divorced; and the conjugal condition of the remainder was unknown. The average size of a family was 4.9 persons, being somewhat larger than the average for the country.

Of persons 10 years old and upward, practically one-half, or exactly 49.8 per cent, were engaged in gainful occupations. Of males, 79.0 per cent were wage-earners; of females, 21.0 per cent. The following table shows the proportion of the wage-earners employed in each of the five general classes of occupations:

Division of wage-earners according to occupations.

	Per cent.
Agriculture	20.8
Professions	4.2
Domestic and personal service	26.1
Trade and transportation	19.9
Manufacturing and mining	29.0

Agriculture is one of the leading occupations. In 1900 the State contained 46,021 farms, of which seven-eighths were occupied by white farmers and one-eighth by negro farmers. Two-thirds of the farms were owned by their occupants, and one-third were rented, either for money rental or on shares of the products. The farms had a total area of 5,170,075 acres. The cultivated area amounted to 3,516,352 acres, or more than two-thirds of the farm area and 55.7 per cent of the total area of the State. The average size of the farms was 112.4 acres, being considerably less than the average for the United States. The total value of all the farms was $204,645,407, which was made up of the following items:

Value of farm lands, buildings, and accessories.

Land	$120,367,550
Buildings	54,810,760
Implements and machinery	8,611,220
Live stock	20,855,877
Average value per farm	4,448
Average value of products per farm	952

The product amounted to 21.0 per cent of the value of the farms, and may be regarded as the farming profit. The following table shows the amount of live stock in the State:

Live stock in Maryland in 1900.

Cattle	306,710
Horses	188,726
Mules	19,734
Sheep	194,079
Swine	359,812

The following table shows the leading farm products:

Dairy products of Maryland in 1900.

Dairy products	$5,228,698
Poultry products	$1,158,020
Fruit	$2,490,385
Corn bushels	19,766,510
Wheat do	9,671,800
Oats do	1,109,560
Potatoes do	1,991,357
Sweet potatoes do	677,848
Hay tons	507,042
Tobacco pounds	24,589,480

In the production of tobacco, Maryland is the eighth State in the Union.

Manufactures are of great importance, Maryland being the fourteenth State in the Union, while in agriculture it is only the twenty-ninth. The following table summarizes its manufactures, of which two-thirds are carried on in the city of Baltimore:

Statistics of manufactures of Maryland for 1900.

Establishments	9,879
Employees	108,325
Horsepower	141,879
Capital	$163,147,260
Wages	$38,748,551
Materials	$144,397,680
Products	$242,552,990

The railway mileage in the State in 1902 was 1,383 miles, most of which was in the Baltimore and Ohio and the Pennsylvania systems. There is one canal, the Chesapeake and Ohio, which follows Potomac River from Cumberland to Washington, D. C., and is principally used for the transportation of coal from the Cumberland district.

The principal and almost sole mineral product of the State is coal, which is mined in large quantities in the neighborhood of Cumberland. It is a bituminous coal of excellent quality. In 1901 the amount mined was 5,113,127 tons.

GAZETTEER.

Aaron; run, a small branch of Savage River in Garrett County.

Abbey; point in Harford County, projecting into the mouth of Bush River.

Abell; post village in St. Mary County.

Aberdeen; creek, a small branch of South River in Anne Arundel County.

Aberdeen; post village in Harford County on the Baltimore and Ohio and the Philadelphia, Baltimore and Washington railroads. Population 600.

Abingdon; post village in Harford County.

Accident; post village in Garrett County.

Accokeek; post village in Prince George County.

Acre; creek, a small branch of Big Annemessex River in Somerset County.

Adam; small, almost entirely marshy island in Chesapeake Bay, Dorchester County.

Adamstown; post village in Frederick County on the Baltimore and Ohio Railroad.

Adelina; post village in Calvert County.

Adkins; small pond drained by Givens Branch in Wicomico County.

Admiral; post village in Anne Arundel County.

Ady; village in Harford County.

Aikin; post village in Cecil County on the Baltimore and Ohio Railroad.

Aireys; post village in Dorchester County on the Philadelphia, Baltimore and Washington Railroad.

Aisquith; neck, small strip of land in Dorchester County, lying between Far Creek and Honga River.

Alberton; post village in Howard County on the Baltimore and Ohio Railroad.

Aldino; post village in Harford County.

Aleck; pond, a small inlet of Isle of Wight Bay in Worcester County.

Alesia; post village in Carroll County on the Western Maryland Railroad.

Allegany; county, in the western mountainous part of the State, limited on the south by Potomac River, the south boundary of the State, on the north by Mason and Dixon's line, which is the southern boundary of the State of Pennsylvania, on the east by Washington County, and on the west by Garrett County. The surface is an alternation of ridges and valleys, trending nearly northeast and southwest, the latter drained by streams flowing into Potomac River. The area of the county is 432 square miles, of which more than one-fourth, or 75,900 acres, was under cultivation in 1900. The population for the same year was 53,694. The county seat and chief city is Cumberland, a coal-mining center of much importance, with a population of 17,128 in 1900. The average magnetic declination in the county in 1900 was 4° 5′ west. The annual rainfall commonly ranges between 45 and 50 inches and the mean annual temperature between 45° and 50°.

Allegany; post village in Allegany County on the Cumberland and Pennsylvania Railroad.

Allegany Grove; village in Allegany County.

Allegany Heights; summit of Backbone Mountain in Garrett County; height, 3,187 feet.

Allen; village in Wicomico County.

10

Allen Fresh; village in Charles County.

Allibone; village in Harford County.

Allomay; creek, heads in Pennsylvania and flows through Carroll County into the Monocacy River.

Almshouse; creek, small branch of South River in Anne Arundel County.

Alpha; post village in Howard County.

Altamont; post village in Garrett County on the Baltimore and Ohio Railroad.

Ambrose; run, a small branch of Cherry Run in Garrett County.

American Corners; post village in Caroline County.

Ammendale; post village in Prince George County on the Baltimore and Ohio Railroad.

Amos; falls, in Susquehanna River in Cecil and Harford counties.

Amos; small island in Susquehanna River in Harford County.

Amos; post village in Harford County.

Anacostia; river, rising in Prince George County and flowing through the District of Columbia into Potomac River.

Andersontown; post village in Caroline County.

Andora; post village in Cecil County.

Annapolis; city and the capital of the State, situated in Anne Arundel County on the Annapolis, Washington and Baltimore and the Baltimore and Annapolis Short Line railroads. Population, 8,525.

Annapolis Harbor; small inlet of Severn River in Anne Arundel County.

Annapolis Junction; station in Howard County on the Annapolis, Washington and Baltimore and the Baltimore and Ohio railroads.

Annapolis Roads; a small inlet of Chesapeake Bay in Anne Arundel County.

Anne Arundel; county, situated in the central part of the State, bounded on the north by Baltimore County, east by Chesapeake Bay, south by Calvert County, west by Patuxent River and Prince George County, and northwest by Howard County. The surface is of a rolling character, but has no very elevated points. The area of the county is 425 square miles, of which more than one-half, or 148,325 acres, was under cultivation in 1900. The county seat and largest city is Annapolis, the capital and oldest city in the State, with a population of 8,525 in 1900. The average magnetic declination in the county in 1900 was 5° 0′ west. The annual rainfall commonly ranges between 45 and 50 inches, and the mean annual temperature between 45° and 50°.

Antietam; river, a branch of Potomac River in Washington County.

Ape Hole; creek, small stream flowing into Pocomoke Sound in Somerset County.

Applegarth; post village on Hooper Island in Dorchester County.

Appleton; post village in Cecil County.

Aquasco; post village in Prince George County.

Araby; post village in Frederick County on the Baltimore and Ohio Railroad.

Arbutus; station in Baltimore County on the Philadelphia, Baltimore and Washington Railroad.

Arden; post village in Somerset County on the New York, Philadelphia and Norfolk Railroad.

Ardwick; post village in Prince George County on the Philadelphia, Baltimore and Washington Railroad.

Arlington; station on the Western Maryland Railroad, partly in Baltimore County and partly in Baltimore City limits.

Armiger; post village in Anne Arundel County.

Arnold; point in Cecil County, projecting into Elk River.

Arnold; point in Anne Arundel County, projecting into Severn River.

Arnold; post village in Anne Arundel County on the Baltimore and Annapolis Short Line Railroad.

Arundel; station in Prince George County on the Philadelphia, Baltimore and Washington Railroad.

Arundel-on-the-Bay; post village in Anne Arundel County.

Ash; post village in Washington County.

Asher Glade; village in Garrett County.

Ashland; post village in Baltimore County.

Ashton; post village in Montgomery County.

Aspen; post village in Montgomery County.

Assacorkin; small marshy island in Chincoteague Bay, Worcester County.

Assawoman; bay, the northern extension of Isle of Wight Bay, which lies between the main coast and an outlying sand bar in Worcester County.

Athaloo; landing on Nanticoke River in Wicomico County.

Atholton; post village in Howard County.

Avalon; post village in Talbot County.

Avalon; station in Baltimore County on the Baltimore and Ohio Railroad.

Avenel; post village in Montgomery County.

Avery; post village in Montgomery County.

Avilton; post village in Garrett County.

Avon; creek, a small branch of Nanjemoy Creek in Charles County.

Avondale; creek, a small branch of Little Run in Carroll County.

Avondale; post village in Carroll County on the Western Maryland Railroad.

Aydelotte; branch, a small stream flowing into Newhope Pond, an inlet of Pocomoke River.

Ayer; creek, a small branch of Trappe Creek in Worcester County.

Bachelor; point in Talbot County, projecting into Tred Avon River.

Back; small branch of Western Branch in Prince George County.

Back; cove, a small inlet of Chesapeake Bay in Smith Island, Somerset County.

Back; creek, a small branch of Choptank River in Dorchester County.

Back; creek, a branch of Elk River in Cecil County.

Back; creek, a small branch of Manoken River in Somerset County.

Back; creek, a small branch of Patapsco River in Anne Arundel County.

Back; creek, a small branch of Patuxent River in Calvert County.

Back; creek, a small branch of Sassafras River in Cecil County.

Back; creek, a small branch of Severn River in Anne Arundel County.

Back; creek, a small stream in Worcester County flowing into Assawoman Bay.

Back; river, a short estuary on the west side of Chesapeake Bay in Baltimore County.

Backbone; mountain in Garrett County.

Back Creek; neck, a narrow strip of land lying between Back Creek and Elk River in Cecil County.

Backgarden; creek, a small stream flowing through sea marshes in Dorchester County into Fishing Bay.

Backgarden; small pond at the head of Backgarden Creek in Dorchester County.

Back River; neck, a strip of land lying between Middle River and Back River in Baltimore County.

Back Wye; river, a branch of Wye River in Queen Anne County.

Bacon Hall; village in Baltimore County.

Bacon Hill; post village in Cecil County on the Philadelphia, Baltimore and Washington Railroad.

Bacons; wharf on St. Mary River in St. Mary County.

Baden; post village in Prince George County.

Bagley; post village in Harford County.

Bakers; cove, a small inlet of Chesapeake Bay in Cecil County.

Bald Friar; village in Cecil County.

Bald Hill; small branch of Western Branch in Prince George County.

Baldwin; post village in Baltimore County on the Maryland and Pennsylvania Railroad.

Baldwin; post village in Cecil County on the Baltimore and Ohio Railroad.

Ball; creek, a small branch of Broad Creek in Talbot County.

Ballanger; creek, a small branch of Monocacy River in Frederick County.

Baltimore; chief city of Maryland, situated on an excellent harbor in Chesapeake Bay. The city is independent of county government. It is entered by the following railroads: Northern Central; Philadelphia, Baltimore and Washington; Baltimore and Annapolis Short Line; Baltimore and Ohio; Western Maryland; and Maryland and Pennsylvania. Population, 508,957.

Baltimore; county, situated in the northern central part of the State, bordered on the north by Pennsylvania, east by Harford County, west by Carroll County, and southwest and south by Patapsco River. This county is the most important one in the State, owing to its position surrounding Baltimore City. The surface is very uneven and varied. The area of the county is 656 square miles, more than one-half of which, or 244,806 acres, was under cultivation in 1900. The population for the same year was 90,755; the county seat, Towson, a town within a short distance of Baltimore City. The average magnetic declination in the county in 1900 was 5° 20′ west. The annual rainfall commonly ranges between 45 and 50 inches, and the mean annual temperature between 50° and 55°.

Bank; post village in Cecil County on the Philadelphia, Baltimore and Washington Railroad.

Barclay; post village in Queen Anne County on the Philadelphia, Baltimore and Washington Railroad.

Barksdale; post village in Cecil County on the Baltimore and Ohio Railroad.

Barley; creek, a small branch of South River in Anne Arundel County.

Barnes; cove, a small inlet of Tangier Sound on Smith Island in Somerset County.

Barnes Landing; creek, a small branch on Smith Island in Somerset County flowing into Chesapeake Bay.

Barnesville; post village in Montgomery County on the Baltimore and Ohio Railroad.

Barrelville; village in Allegany County on the Cumberland and Pennsylvania Railroad.

Barren; creek, a branch of Nanticoke River in Wicomico County.

Barron; island in Dorchester County in Chesapeake Bay.

Barron Creek; point in Dorchester County, projecting into Nanticoke River.

Barron Neck; point in Talbot County, projecting into Harris Creek.

Barstow; post village in Calvert County.

Bartholows; post village in Frederick County on the Baltimore and Ohio Railroad.

Bartlett; run, a small stream rising in Garrett County and flowing through Allegany County into Georges Creek.

Barton; post village in Allegany County on the Cumberland and Pennsylvania Railroad.

Basin; run, a small branch of Octararo Creek in Cecil County.

Basket Switch; village in Worcester County on the Philadelphia, Baltimore and Washington Railroad.

Bassett; creek, a small branch flowing into Newport Bay from Worcester County.

Bats; neck, a strip of land lying between Warehouse and Shipping creeks in Queen Anne County.

Battle; creek, a small branch of Patuxent River in Calvert County.

Battle; post village in Calvert County.

Bay; village in Carroll County.

Bayard; post village in Anne Arundel County.

Bay Bush; point in Kent County, projecting into Chester River.

Baynesville; post village in Baltimore County.

Bay Ridge; village in Anne Arundel County on the Bay Ridge Railroad.

Bayview; village in Cecil County.

Bayview, village in Worcester County.

Bay View Junction; station in Baltimore County on the Baltimore and Ohio and the Philadelphia, Baltimore and Washington railroads.

Beach; point in Harford County, projecting into Bush River.

Beacon Clumps; group of small marshy islands in Chincoteague Bay in Worcester County.

Beaghn; small branch of Beaverdam Creek in Wicomico County.

Beallsville; post village in Montgomery County.

Beallsville; village in Frederick County.

Beane; post village in Montgomery County.

Beantown; village in Charles County.

Bear; small branch of Big Pipe Creek in Carroll County.

Bear; creek, a small branch of Patapsco River in Baltimore County.

Bear; creek, a small stream rising in Pennsylvania and flowing through Washington County into Sideling Hill Creek.

Bear; creek, a branch of Youghiogheny River in Garrett County.

Bear; hill, a summit of Fourmile Ridge in Garrett County.

Bear; hollow in Warrior Mountain in Allegany County.

Bear; point in Harford County, projecting into Chesapeake Bay.

Bear Cabin; small branch of Winters Run in Hartford County.

Bear Camp; branch, a small stream rising in Pennsylvania and flowing through Allegany County into Fifteenmile Creek.

Bear Pen; run, a small branch of Savage River in Garrett County.

Beard; creek, a small branch of South River in Anne Arundel County.

Beaver; run, a small branch of North Branch of Patapsco River in Carroll County.

Beavercreek; post village in Washington County.

Beaver Dam; creek, a branch of Gunpowder Falls in Baltimore County.

Beaver Dam; creek, a small branch of Tuckahoe Creek in Queen Anne County.

Beaverdam; creek, a branch of Wicomico River in Wicomico County.

Beaverdam; creek, a small stream flowing into Keene Broads, a small pond at the head of St. John Creek in Dorchester County.

Beaverdam; creek, a small branch of Anacostia River in Prince George County.

Beaverdam; creek, a small branch of Blackwater River in Dorchester County.

Beaverdam; creek, a small branch of Chicacomico Creek in Dorchester County.

Beaverdam; creek, a small branch of Nassawango Creek in Wicomico County.

Beaverdam; creek, a small branch of Point Branch in Prince George County.

Beaverdam; post village in Worcester County on the New York, Philadelphia and Norfolk Railroad.

Beavue; post village in St. Mary County.

Beck; small branch of Beaverdam Creek in Prince George County.

Beckleysville; village in Baltimore County.

Beckman; post village in Garrett County.

Beckwith; creek, a small branch of Choptank River in Dorchester County.

Bed; run, a small branch of Gwynn Falls in Baltimore County.

Bedsworth; post village in Somerset County.

Beetree; small branch of Gunpowder Falls in Baltimore County.

Beir; village in Allegany County on the Baltimore and Ohio and the West Virginia Central and Pittsburg railroads.

Belair; county seat of Harford County on the Maryland and Pennsylvania Railroad. Population 961.

Belalton; post village in Charles County.

Belcamp; post village in Harford County on the Baltimore and Ohio Railroad.

Belfast; village in Baltimore County.

Bellegrove; post village in Allegany County.

Bell Mills; village in Montgomery County.

Bellevue; village in Talbot County.

Beltsville; station in Prince George County on the Baltimore and Ohio Railroad.

Belvidere; village in Cecil County on the Baltimore and Ohio Railroad.

Ben; run, a small branch of Patapsco River in Baltimore County.

Benedict; post village in Charles County.

Benevola; post village in Washington County.

Benfield; post village in Anne Arundel County.

Bengies; point in Baltimore County, projecting into Saltpeter Creek.

Bengies; post village in Baltimore County on the Philadelphia, Baltimore and Washington Railroad.

Bennett; creek, a small branch of Monocacy River in Frederick County.

Bennett; point in Anne Arundel County, projecting into Miles Creek.

Benoni; point in Talbot County, projecting into Choptank River.

Bens; creek, a small branch of Lingamore Creek in Frederick County.

Benson; post village in Harford County.

Bentley; cove, a small inlet of Honga River in Dorchester County.

Bentley; point in Dorchester County on Hooper Island, projecting into Honga River.

Bentley; station in Baltimore County on the Northern Central Railway.

Bentley Springs; post village in Baltimore County on Northern Central Railway.

Benville; village in Charles County.

Benville; village in St. Mary County.

Berean; village in Baltimore County.

Berkley; post village in Harford County.

Berlin; town in Worcester County on the Baltimore, Chesapeake and Atlantic and the Philadelphia, Baltimore and Washington railroads.   Population, 1,246.

Berrett; village in Carroll County.

Bertha; village in Calvert County.

Berwyn; post village in Prince George County on the Baltimore and Ohio Railroad.

Bestpitch; post village in Dorchester County.

Betheden Church; village in Worcester County.

Bethel; village in Somerset County.

Bethesda; post village in Montgomery County.

Beth Gap; village in Anne Arundel County.

Bethlehem; post village in Caroline County on the Baltimore, Chesapeake and Atlantic Railway.

Betterton; post village in Kent County.

Bevansville; post village in Garrett County.

Bier; post village in Allegany County on the Baltimore and Ohio and the West Virginia Central and Pittsburg railroads.

Big; small island in Worcester County in Assawoman Bay.

Big; small pond in Worcester County drained by Swan Gut Creek.

Big; ridge, a spur of Town Hill in Allegany County.

Big; run, a small branch of Maple Run in Allegany County.

Big; run, a small branch of Savage Creek in Garrett County.

Big Annemessex; river in Somerset County flowing into Tangier Sound.

Big Bay; point in Worcester County, projecting into Chincoteague Bay.

Big Branch; creek, a small branch of Deer Creek in Harford County.

Big Elk; creek, heads in Pennsylvania and flows through Cecil County into **Elk** River.

Big Laurel; run, a tributary of South Branch of Castleman River in Garrett County.

Big Monie; creek, a tributary to Chesapeake Bay in Somerset County.

Big Patuxent; river, heading in Howard County and flowing southeast into Chesapeake Bay, forming an estuary in its lower course.

Big Piney; run, heads in Garrett County and flows through Pennsylvania into Castleman River.

Bigpool; post village in Washington County on the Western Maryland Railroad.

Big Savage; mountain, lies between Savage River and Georges Creek in Garrett County.

Big Shade; run, heads in Pennsylvania and flows through Garrett County into Castleman River.

Bigspring; post village in Washington County.

Big Thorofare; water passageway in Somerset County between Smith Island and Otter Island.

Billiard; point in St. Mary County, projecting into Patuxent River.

Billy; small marshy island in Chesapeake Bay in Dorchester County.

Binum; run, a small branch of Bush Creek in Harford County.

Birch; small branch of Shingle Landing Prong in Worcester County.

Bird Hill; post village in Carroll County.

Bird; river, a tributary of Gunpowder River in Baltimore County.

Birdsville; post village in Anne Arundel County.

Birdtown; village in Somerset County.

Biscoe; creek, a small branch of Potomac River in St. Mary County.

Bishop; post village in Worcester County on the Philadelphia, Baltimore and Washington Railroad.

Bishop Head; point in Dorchester County, projecting into Fishing Bay and Hooper Strait.

Bishop Head; village in Dorchester County.

Bishopville; post village in Worcester County.   Population 243.

Bittinger; post village in Garrett County.

Bivalve; post village in Wicomico County.

Black; creek, a small branch flowing into Knapp Narrows in Talbot County.

Black; hill in Cecil County.   Elevation, 311 feet.

Blackhawk; run, a small branch of Middle Fork Creek in Garrett County.

Blackhorse; village in Harford County.

Blacklick; run, a small tributary of Savage River in Garrett County.

Blackrock; run, a small branch of Western Branch in Baltimore County.

Blacks; post village in Kent County.

Black Swamp; creek, a small branch of Patuxent River in Prince George County.

Blackwalnut; cove, a small inlet of Choptank River in Talbot County.

Blackwalnut; creek, a small tributary to Chesapeake Bay in Anne Arundel County.

Blackwalnut; point in Talbot County, projecting into mouth of Choptank River

Blackwater; river in Dorchester County flowing through sea marshes into Fishing Bay.

Bladensburg; town in Prince George County on the Baltimore and Ohio Railroad. Population, 463.

Blake; creek, a small tributary of Potomac River in St. Mary County.

Blake; post village in Cecil County.

Blakistone; post village in St. Mary County.

Blakistone; small island in Potomac River in St. Mary County.   A light-house is erected thereon.

Blenheim; post village in Baltimore County.

Blocktown; village in Montgomery County.

Bloodsworth; island almost entirely marshy in Chesapeake Bay, Dorchester County.

Bloody Point; creek, a small tributary to Chesapeake Bay in Talbot County.

Bloomfield; village in Talbot County on the Baltimore, Chesapeake and Atlantic Railway.

Blooming Rose Settlement; village in Garrett County.

Bloomington; post village in Garrett County on the Baltimore and Ohio Railroad.

Blossom; hill, a summit in Garrett County between Pine Hill and Solomon Ridge.

Blue; pond, an inlet of Chincoteague Bay in Worcester County.

Blueball; post village in Cecil County.

Bluelick; run, a small tributary of Savage River in Garrett County.

Blue Mount; station in Baltimore County on the Northern Central Railway.

Blue Mountain; post village in Washington County on the Western Maryland Railroad.

Bluestone; post village in St. Mary County.

Bluff; point in Anne Arundel County, projecting into Severn River.

Bluff; point in St. Mary County, projecting into Wicomico River.

Bluff; point on Hooper Island in Dorchester County, projecting into Chesapeake Bay.

Blythedale; post village in Cecil County.

Boar; small island in Assawoman Bay in Worcester County.

Boat; small marshy island in Lighting Knot Cove in Somerset County, south of Smith Island.

Bodkin; creek, a small tributary of Patapsco River in Anne Arundel County.

Bodkin; small island in Eastern Bay in Queen Anne County.

Bodkin; point in Anne Arundel County, projecting into Chesapeake Bay.

Bohemia; river, a tributary to Elk River in Cecil County.

Bolingbroke; creek, a small tributary of Choptank River in Talbot County.

Bolivar; village in Frederick County.

Booby; small island in Chesapeake Bay in Baltimore County.

Boone; creek, a small tributary of Choptank River in Talbot County.

Boones; village in Anne Arundel County.

Boonsboro; town in Washington County. Population, 700.

Boothbyhill; post village in Harford County.

Booxe; ditch, a small branch of Blackwater River in Dorchester County.

Boring; post village in Baltimore County.

Bosely; village in Baltimore County.

Bostetter; post village in Washington County.

Boston; creek, a small branch of Patuxent River in St. Mary County.

Bowens; post village in Calvert County.

Bowie; town in Prince George County on the Philadelphia, Baltimore and Washington Railroad. Population, 443.

Bowley Bar; point in Baltimore County, projecting into Middle River.

Box; point in Kent County, projecting into Chester River.

Boxiron; creek, a small branch flowing into Chincoteague Bay in Worcester County.

Boxiron; village in Worcester County.

Boyer; knob, a summit in Polish Mountain in Allegany County. Height, 1,564 feet.

Boyds; post village in Montgomery County on the Baltimore and Ohio Railroad.

Bozman; post village in Talbot County.

Braddock; run, a small tributary of North Branch of Potomac River in Allegany County.

Bradenbaugh; village in Harford County.

Bradshaw; post village in Baltimore County on the Baltimore and Ohio Railroad.

Brady; station in Allegany County on the Baltimore and Ohio Railroad.

Branchville; post village in Prince George County on the Baltimore and Ohio Railroad.

Brandywine; post village in Prince George County on the Philadelphia, Baltimore and Washington Railroad.

Bread and Cheese; creek, a small branch of Back River in Baltimore County.

Break; point in Queen Anne County, projecting into Chester River.

Breakneck; hill, a summit in Martin Mountain in Allegany County. Height, 1,872 feet.

Breathedsville; post village in Washington County.

Brentland; post village in Charles County.

Brentwood; post village in Prince George County on the Baltimore and Ohio Railroad.

Breton; bay, an inlet of Potomac River in St. Mary County.

Brewer; creek, a small tributary of Severn River in Anne Arundel County.

Brewer; point in Anne Arundel County, projecting into Severn River.

Brewington; branch, a small tributary of Wicomico River in Wicomico County.

Brew Mahr Mill; village in Garrett County.

Brian; point in Queen Anne County, projecting into Prospect Bay.

Briary; creek, a small branch of Harris Creek in Talbot County.

Brice; point in Anne Arundel County, projecting into Severn River.

Brice; run, a small tributary of Patapsco River in Baltimore County.

Brice; village in Charles County.

Bricoe; wharf on the Patuxent River in St. Mary County.

Bridge; creek, a small branch of Broad Creek in Talbot County.

Bridgetown; town in Caroline County. Population, 50.

Brien; run, a small branch of Northeast Creek in Baltimore County.

Brier; point in Baltimore County, projecting into Chesapeake Bay.

Brier; mountain ridge in Garrett County.

Briery; point in Harford County, projecting into Bush Creek.

Brighton; post village in Montgomery County.

Brightseat; village in Prince George County.

Brink; post village in Montgomery County.

Brinklow; post village in Montgomery County.

Bristol; post village in Anne Arundel County.

Broad; creek, a small branch flowing into Chesapeake Bay in Queen Anne County.

Broad; creek, a small branch flowing into Ellis Bay in Wicomico County.

Broad; creek, a small stream flowing into Pocomoke Sound in Somerset County.

Broad; creek, a small tributary of Chester River in Kent County.

Broad; creek, a small tributary of Magothy River in Anne Arundel County.

Broad; creek, a small tributary of Manokin River in Somerset County.

Broad; creek, a small tributary of South River in Anne Arundel County.

Broad; creek, a tributary of Choptank River in Talbot County.

Broad; creek, a tributary of Susquehanna River in Harford County.

Broad; run, a small branch of James Creek in Harford County.

Broad; run, a small tributary of Gunpowder Falls in Baltimore County.

Broad; run, a small tributary of Potomac River in Montgomery County.

Broad; neck, a strip of land between East and West forks of Langford Bay in Kent County.

Broad Ford; run, a small tributary of Little Youghiogheny River in Garrett County.

Broad Run; village in Frederick County.

Brockatonorton; bay, an arm of Chincoteague Bay in Worcester County.

Brome; wharf, on St. Mary River in St. Mary County.

Bronnack; bay, an inlet of Trippe Bay in Dorchester County.

Brook; run, a small branch of McIntosh Run, in St. Mary County.

Brookeville; town in Montgomery County. Population, 158.

Brooklandville; post village in Baltimore County on the Northern Central Railway.

Brooklyn; station in Anne Arundel County on the Baltimore and Ohio Railroad.

Brooks; creek, a small branch of Little Choptank River in Dorchester County.

Brookview; post village in Dorchester County on the Baltimore, Chesapeake and Atlantic Railway.

Broome; small, almost entirely marshy island in Patuxent River in Calvert County.

Broome Island; post village in Calvert County.

Browning Mill; village in Garrett County.

Browningsville; village in Montgomery County.

Browns; creek, a small tributary of Chester River in Kent County.

Browns; creek, a small stream flowing into Hawk Cove in Baltimore County.

Browns; landing on the Wye River in Queen Anne County.

Browns; point in Baltimore County, projecting into Middle River.

Brownsville; post village in Washington County on the Baltimore and Ohio Railroad.

Bruff; island in Wye River in Talbot County.

Brunswick; town in Frederick County on the Baltimore and Ohio Railroad. Population, 2,471.

Bryantown; post village in Charles County.

Bryanville; village in Garrett County.

Buck; hill, a summit in Peapatch Ridge in Garrett County.

Buckeystown; post village in Frederick County on the Baltimore and Ohio Railroad.

Buckingham; landing on Chester River in Kent County.

Buck Island; pond, a small inlet of St. Martin River in Worcester County.

Bucklodge; post village in Montgomery County on the Baltimore and Ohio Railroad.

Buck Neck; landing on Worton Creek in Kent County.

Bucktown; post village in Dorchester County.

Budd; landing on Sassafras River in Cecil County.

Budd; creek, a small stream on the boundary between St. Mary County and Charles County, flowing into Wicomico River.

Budd Creek; landing on Wicomico River in Charles County.

Budd Creek; post village in St. Mary County.

Buenavista; post village in Calvert County.

Buenavista; village in Prince George County.

Buffalo; creek, a small branch of Piney Creek in Baltimore County.

Buffalo; run, a small branch of Youghiogeny River in Garrett County.

Bull Glade; run, a small branch of Muddy Run in Garrett County.

Bull Mountain; hill in Cecil County. Height, 306 feet.

Bullock; small island at mouth of Wicomico River in St. Mary County.

Burch; post village in Calvert County.

Burdette; post village in Montgomery County.

Burkittsville; town in Frederick County. Population, 229.

Burnt Mill; creek, small branch of McIntosh Run in St. Mary County

Burnt Mills; post village in Montgomery County.

Burrissville; village in Queen Anne County.

Burrsville; post village in Caroline County.

Burtonsville; post village in Montgomery County.

Bush; creek, a small branch of Monocacy River in Frederick County.

Bush; point in Harford County, projecting into Bush River.

Bush; ridge, a spur of Collier Mountain in Allegany County.

Bush Cabin; small branch of Gunpowder Falls in Baltimore County.

Bush River; post village in Harford County on the Philadelphia, Baltimore and Washington Railroad.

Bushwood; village in St. Mary County.

Butler; post village in Baltimore County.

Butlers; village in Anne Arundel County.

Butlertown; village in Kent County.

Buxton; village in Prince George County.

Buzzard Island; creek, a small tributary of Patuxent River in Calvert County.

Cabin; small branch of Little Seneca Creek in Montgomery County.

Cabin; small branch of Severn River in Anne Arundel County.

Cabin; small branch of Western Branch in Prince George County.

Cabin; branch, a small tributary of Patuxent River in Howard County.

Cabin; creek, a small stream flowing into Curtis Bay in Anne Arundel County.

Cabin; creek, a small stream flowing into Prospect Bay in Queen Anne County.

Cabin; creek, a small tributary of Choptank River in Dorchester County.

Cabin Creek; neck, a strip of land lying between Blinthorn and Cabin creeks in Dorchester County.

Cabin John; creek, a small tributary of Potomac River in Montgomery County.

Cabin John; creek, a small tributary of Elk River in Cecil County.

Cabin John; post village in Montgomery County.

Cadle; creek, a small tributary of Rhode River in Anne Arundel County.

California; post village in St. Mary County.

California; post village in Wicomico County.

Calvary; post village in Harford County.

Calvert; bay, a small arm of Potomac River in St. Mary County.

Calvert; county, situated in the western shore of the Chesapeake Bay, forming a peninsula which is bounded on the north by Anne Arundel County, east by the bay, and west by Patuxent River. The surface is undulating and drains from a central elevation toward the bay and river, into which flow many small creeks. The area of the county is 222 square miles, of which nearly two-thirds, or 88,605 acres, were under cultivation in 1900. The population for the same year was 10,223; the county seat, Prince Fredericktown. The average magnetic declination in the county in 1900 was 4° 45′ west. The annual rainfall commonly ranges between 45 and 50 inches, and the mean annual temperature between 50° and 55°.

Calvert; creek, a small stream in St. Mary County flowing into Calvert Bay.

Calvert; post village in Cecil County.

Calverton; station within the chartered limits of Baltimore City on the Philadelphia, Baltimore and Washington Railroad.

Cambria; station in Harford County on the Maryland and Pennsylvania Railroad.

Cambridge; town in Dorchester County on the Philadelphia, Baltimore and Washington Railroad. Population, 5,747.

Camden; village in Wicomico County.

Camden Junction; village in Baltimore County.

Campbell; post village in Worcester County.

Campbell Ditch; run, a small branch of Aydelotte Branch in Wicomico County.

Campsprings; post village in Prince George County.

Canal; village in Cecil County.

Canoe Neck; creek, a small branch of St. Clement Creek in St. Mary County.

Canton; town in Baltimore County near Baltimore.

Capitola; post village in Wicomico County.

Captain; point in St. Mary County, projecting into Patuxent River.

Cardiff; post village in Harford County on the Maryland and Pennsylvania Railroad.

Carea; post village in Harford County.

Caren; village in Harford County.

Carey; creek, a small tributary of Choptank River in Dorchester County.

Carey; run, a small tributary of Savage River in Garrett County.

Carlos Junction; station in Allegany County on the Cumberland and Pennsylvania Railroad.

Carmichael; post village in Queen Anne County.

Carny; post village in Baltimore County.

Caroline; county, bounded on the east by the State of Delaware, northwest and west by Queen Anne and Talbot counties, and south by Dorchester County. The surface is generally level, though sufficiently undulating to afford good drainage. The area is 320 square miles, of which more than two-thirds, or 125,908 acres, were under cultivation in 1900. The population for the same year was 16,248; county seat, Denton. The average magnetic declination in the county in 1900 was 5° 45' west. The annual rainfall commonly ranges between 45 and 50 inches, and the mean annual temperature between 50° and 55°.

Carpenter; small island in Chester River in Queen Anne County.

Carpenter; point in Cecil County, projecting into Chesapeake Bay.

Carr; creek, a small stream flowing into Annapolis Roads in Anne Arundel County.

Carroll; branch, a small tributary of Gunpowder Falls in Baltimore County.

Carroll; county, bounded on the north by Pennsylvania, south by Howard County, east by Baltimore County, and west by Frederick County. The surface is mostly undulating, watered by fine streams, tributaries of Patapsco and Monocacy rivers, which flow from many springs of the purest water. The area of the county is 437 square miles, of which more than three-fourths, or 227,693 acres, were under cultivation in 1900. The population for the same year was 33,860. The county seat and chief town is Westminster, a town of about 3,200 inhabitants. The magnetic declination in the county in 1900 was 5° 30' west. The annual rainfall in the county commonly ranges between 45 and 50 inches and the mean annual temperature between 50° and 55°.

Carroll; creek, a small tributary of Monocacy River in Frederick County.

Carroll; point in Baltimore County, projecting into Bush River.

Carrollton; post village in Carroll County on the Western Maryland Railroad.

Carrot; cove, a small inlet of Northeast River in Cecil County.

Carsins; run, a small branch of Swan Creek in Harford County.

Carsins; village in Harford County.

Carter; creek, a small stream flowing into Chesapeake Bay in Queen Anne County.

Carthagena; creek, a small tributary of St. Mary River in St. Mary County.

Carville; station in Queen Anne County on the Philadelphia, Baltimore and Washington Railroad.

Cascade; post village in Washington County.

Cassidy; wharf on Sassafras River in Cecil County.

Casson; neck, a strip of land between Hudson and Phillips creeks in Dorchester County.

Castlehaven; village in Dorchester County.

Castleman; river heading in Garrett County and flowing into Pennsylvania into Youghiogheny River.

Castleton; post village in Harford County.

Cat; creek, a small tributary of Patuxent River in St. Mary County.

Cathcart; village in Harford County.

Catlin; village in Queen Anne County.

Catoctin; creek, a tributary of Potomac River in Frederick County.

Catoctin; mountain, a continuation of Catoctin Mountain in Virginia into Frederick County.

Catoctin; station in Frederick County on the Baltimore and Ohio Railroad.

Catonsville; village in Baltimore County.

Cavetown; post village in Washington County on the Western Maryland Railroad.

Cayots; post village in Cecil County.

Cecil; county, organized in 1647, one of the most thriving and enterprising in the State. It is situated in the northeast corner of the State, bounded on the north by Pennsylvania, east by Delaware, south by Sassafras River and west by Chesapeake Bay and Susquehanna River. The surface is of a mixed character, that part above the bay being mostly rolling and hilly, while below Elkton it is level. The area of the county is 360 square miles, of which almost two-thirds, or 141,401 acres were under cultivation in 1900. The population for the same year was 24,662. The county seat is Elkton, a town of about 2,600 inhabitants. Port Deposit is the principal business town, having a population of about 1,600, while Chesapeake City is the third town in size, having a population of about 1,200. The average magnetic declination in 1900 was 4° 45′ west. The annual rainfall ordinarily ranges between 45 and 50 inches and the mean annual temperature between 50° and 55°.

Cecil; creek, a small stream in St. Mary County flowing into St. Clements Bay.

Cecilton; village in Cecil County.

Cedar; creek, a small stream flowing into Fishing Bay in Dorchester County.

Cedar; hill in Harford County.

Cedar; point in Anne Arundel County, projecting into West River.

Cedar; point in Anne Arundel County, projecting into Severn River.

Cedar; point in Charles County, projecting into Potomac River.

Cedar; point in Dorchester County, projecting into Honga River.

Cedar; point in Kent County, projecting into Chester River.

Cedar; point in St. Mary County, projecting into Chesapeake Bay.

Cedar; point in Talbot County, projecting into Broad Bay.

Cedar; point in Worcester County, projecting into St. Martin River.

Cedar; small marshy island in Chincoteague Bay in Worcester County.

Cedar; straits, on the boundary between Somerset County, Md., and Accomac County, Va.

Cedar Cliff; village in Allegany County.

Cedargrove; post village in Montgomery County.

Cedarville; post village in Prince George County on the Washington, Potomac and Chesapeake Railroad.

Centerville; county seat of Queen Anne County. Population, 1,231.

Chalk; point in Anne Arundel County, projecting into West River.

Champ; post village in Somerset County.

Chance; post village in Somerset County.

Chance; point in Talbot County, projecting into Harris Creek.

Chancellor; point in St. Mary County, projecting into St. Mary River.

Chancellor; point in Talbot County, projecting into Choptank River.

Chancellors; point in Dorchester County, projecting into Choptank River.

Chaney; post village in Calvert County on the Chesapeake Beach Railway.

Chaneyville; post village in Calvert County.

Chapel; creek, a small branch of Choptank River in Dorchester County.

Chapel; point in Charles County, projecting into Port Tobacco River.

Chapel; village in Harford County.

Chapters; point in Wicomico County, projecting into Nanticoke River.

Chaptico; bay, an inlet of Wicomico River in St. Mary County.

Chaptico; creek, a small tributary to Chaptico Bay in St. Mary County.

Chaptico; post village in St. Mary County.

Charles; small branch of Western Branch in Prince George County.

Charles; creek, a small branch of Honga River in Dorchester County.

Charles; county, organized in 1640, occupies the southwest part of the State, and is bounded on the west and south by Potomac River, north by Prince George County, and on the southwest by St. Mary County. The surface of the county is generally low, but undulated sufficiently to be well drained by the numerous branches of the bordering rivers. The area of the county is 451 square miles, of which more than one-half, or 153,465 acres, was under cultivation in 1900. The population for the same year was 17,662; the county seat, Laplata. The average magnetic declination in 1900 was 4° 30′ west. The annual rainfall ordinarily ranges between 45 and 50 inches and the mean annual temperature between 50° and 55°.

Charles; point in Somerset County, projecting into Big Annemessex River.

Charles; run, a small tributary of Gunpowder Falls in Baltimore County.

Charleston; creek, a small tributary of Wicomico River in Charles County.

Charlestown; town in Cecil County on the Philadelphia, Baltimore and Washington Railroad. Population, 244.

Charlestown; village in Allegany County.

Charlesville; village in Frederick County.

Charlotte Hall; post village in St. Mary County on the Washington, Potomac and Chesapeake Railroad.

Charlton; post village in Washington County on the Western Maryland Railroad.

Chase; creek, a small tributary of Severn River in Anne Arundle County.

Chase; post village in Baltimore County on the Philadelphia, Baltimore and Washington Railroad.

Chattolanee; post village in Baltimore County.

Chautauqua Beach; post village in Anne Arundel County on the Bay Ridge Railroad.

Cheltenham; post village in Prince George County on the Philadelphia, Baltimore and Washington Railroad.

Cherry; creek, a small branch of Youghiogheny River in Garrett County.

Cherry; creek, a branch of Deep Creek in Garrett County.

Cherry; point in Dorchester County, projecting into Choptank River.

Cherry; small island in Choptank River in Dorchester County.

Cherry Cove; creek, a small stream flowing into Breton Bay in St. Mary County.

Cherryfield; point in St. Mary County, projecting into St. Mary River.

Cherry Glade; run, small tributary of Little Youghiogheny River in Garrett County.

Cherryhill; post village in Cecil County.

Cherry Hill; village in Harford County.

Chesapeake; bay, an arm of the Atlantic Ocean, extending from northeast Maryland nearly south, connecting with the Atlantic Ocean in Virginia, between Capes Charles and Henry. Its length is about 175 miles, and breadth 8 or 10 miles. Into it flow many large rivers from the west, namely, the Susquehanna at its head, the Rappahannock, York, and James. The bay has been produced by the sinking of the land, and the same movement is converting the lower courses of all these rivers into estuaries. The shores of the bay are marshy, especially the east shore, where the country is extremely low.

Chesapeake; town in Cecil County. Population, 1,172.

Chesapeake and Ohio; canal, artificial waterway running parallel with Potomac River from Cumberland, Md., to Georgetown, D. C.

Chesapeake Beach; post village in Calvert County on Chesapeake Beach Railway.

Chester; post village in Queen Anne County on Queen Anne's Railroad.

Chester; river on boundary between Kent and Queen Anne counties tributary to Chesapeake Bay.

Chesterfield; post village in Anne Arundel County.

Chestertown; county seat of Kent County on the Philadelphia, Baltimore and Washington Railroad. Population 3,008.

Chesterville; post village in Kent County.

Chestnut Hill; village in Harford County.

Chestnut Knob; hill in Garrett County 2,500 feet high.

Cheston; creek, small tributary of West River in Anne Arundel County.

Chevy Chase; post village in Montgomery County.

Chew; creek, a small tributary of Patuxent River in Calvert County.

Chewsville; post village in Washington County.

Chicacomico; river, a branch of Transquaking River in Dorchester County.

Chicamuxen; post village in Charles County.

Chickomuxen; creek, a small tributary of Potomac River in Charles County.

Chicono; branch, small tributary of Nanticoke River in Dorchester County.

Chilbury; point in Harford County, projecting into Bush River.

Childs; post village in Cecil County on the Baltimore and Ohio Railroad.

Chillum; post village in Prince George County.

Chincapin; run, a small branch of Herring Run in Baltimore County.

Chincoteague; bay, a shallow lagoon with marshy shores separating the mainland of Worcester County, Md., and Accomac County, Va., from the sand bars of the Atlantic coast.

Chingville; post village in St. Mary County.

Chisholm; run, a small tributary of Youghiogheny River in Garrett County.

Chlora; point in Talbot County, projecting into Choptank River.

Choptank; post village in Caroline County.

Choptank; river, heading in Caroline County and forming part of the boundary between Carroll, Talbot, and Dorchester counties and flowing into Chesapeake Bay.

Christiana; creek, heads in Pennsylvania and flows across the northeastern part of Cecil County, through Delaware into Delaware Bay.

Christley; run, a small tributary of Muddick River in Garrett County.

Christs Rock; village in Dorchester County.

Chromehill; village in Harford County.

Chub; run, heads in Pennsylvania and flows through Garrett County into Mill Run.

Church; creek, a small tributary of Choptank River in Dorchester County.

Church; creek, a small tributary of Bush River in Harford County.

Church; creek, a small tributary of Chester River in Kent County.

Church; creek, a small tributary of South River in Anne Arundel County.

Church; run, a small branch of Piney Run in Garrett County.

Churchcreek; post village in Dorchester County.

Church Hill; town in Queen Anne County.   Population, 368.

Churchton; post village in Anne Arundel County.

Churchville; post village in Harford County.

Churn; creek, a small branch in Kent County flowing into Still Pond.

Clagettsville; village in Montgomery County.

Claiborne; post village in Talbot County.

Clara; post village in Wicomico County.

Clark; point in Baltimore County, projecting into Middle River.

Clark; run, a small stream in Charles County flowing into Zekiah Swamp.

Clark; run, a small branch of Cherry run in Garrett County.

Clarksburg; post village in Montgomery County.

Clarkson; post village in Howard County.

Clarksville; post village in Howard County.

Clarks Wharf; village in Calvert County.

Clarysville; village in Allegany County on the George's Creek and Cumberland Railroad.

Clay; island, a bit of elevated dry land in sea marshes of Dorchester County.

Clay Bank; point in Baltimore County, projecting into Patapsco River.

Clay Island; creek, a bayou flowing through Clay Island in Dorchester County.

Clayton; post village in Harford County on the Baltimore and Ohio Railroad.

Clear Spring; town in Washington County on the Western Maryland Railroad. Population 474.

Clements; creek, a small tributary of Severn River in Anne Arundel County.

Clements; post village in St. Mary County.

Clermont Mills; village in Harford County.

Clifford; station in Baltimore County on the Baltimore and Ohio and Baltimore and Annapolis Short Line railroads.

Clifton; beach in Charles County on Potomac River.

Clifton; small lake in suburb of Baltimore city within its chartered limits.

Clifton; point in Somerset County, projecting into Manokin River.

Clinton; post village in Prince George County.

Cloppers; post village in Montgomery County on the Baltimore and Ohio Railroad.

Cloverly; post village in Montgomery County.

Cobb; point in Charles County, projecting into Wicomico River.

Cockey; small island at mouth of Chester River in Kent County.

Cockeysville; post village in Baltimore County on the Northern Central Railway.

Cocks; point in Anne Arundel County, projecting into Severn River.

Cocktown; creek, a small tributary of Patuxent River in Calvert County.

Coffins; point in Worcester County, projecting into Sinepuxent Bay.

Cohouck; point in St. Mary County, projecting into Wicomico River.

Cokeland; post village in Dorchester County.

Cokesbury; village in Somerset County.

Colbourn; creek, a small stream flowing into Big Annemessex River in Somerset County.

Colbourne; post village in Worcester County.

Cole; creek, a small tributary of Patuxent River in St. Mary County.

Cole; post village in Harford County.

Coleman; post village in Kent County.

Colesville; post village in Montgomery County.

Colgate; creek, a small tributary of Patapsco River in Baltimore County.

College Green; village in Cecil County.

College Park; post village in Prince George County on the Baltimore and Ohio Railroad.

Collier; small marshy island in Isle of Wight Bay in Worcester County.

Collier; small mountain ridge in Allegany County.

Collier; run, a small stream heading in Pennsylvania and flowing through Garrett County into Mill Creek.

Collington; branch of Western Branch in Prince George County.

Collington; post village in Prince George County on the Philadelphia, Baltimore and Washington Railroad.

Collins; gut, a small branch of Wicomico Creek in Wicomico County.

Colora; post village in Cecil County on the Philadelphia, Baltimore and Washington Railroad.

Colton; village in St. Mary County.

Columbia; post village in Howard County.

Combs; creek, a small stream flowing into Breton Bay in St. Mary County.

Comcy; point in Queen Anne County, projecting into Chester River.

Comegy Bight; small island in Chester River in Kent County.

Comegys; run, a small branch of Broad Ford Run in Garrett County.

Compton; post village in St. Mary County.

Comus; post village in Montgomery County.

Conaways; post vi.lage in Anne Arundel County.

Concord; point in Harford County, projecting into Susquehanna River.

Concord; post village in Caroline County.

Conowingo; creek, a stream rising in Pennsylvania and flowing through Cecil County into Susquehanna River.

Contee; station in Prince George County on the Baltimore and Ohio Railroad.

Contrary; knob, a hill in Garrett County.   Height, 2,500 feet.

Conway; hill in Backbone Mountain in Garrett County.   Height, 3,073 feet.

Conwingo; post village in Cecil County.

Cook; point in Dorchester County, projecting into Choptank River.

Cook Point; cove, a small inlet of Choptank River in Dorchester County.

Cooksey; post village in Charles County.

Cooksville; post village in Howard County.

Coolbranch; run, a small branch of Deer Creek in Harford County.

Coon; small mountain ridge in Washington County.

Cooper; creek, a small branch of St. Mary River in St. Mary County.

Cooper; village in Harford County.

Coopstown; village in Harford County.

Copperville; village in Talbot County.

Corbett; post village in Baltimore County on the Northern Central Railway.

Corbin; village in Worcester County.

Cordova; post village in Talbot County on the Philadelphia, Baltimore and Washington Railroad.

Corkers; creek, a tributary of Pocomoke River in Worcester County.

Cormon; point in Somerset County, projecting into Manokin River.

Corners; wharf on Choptank River in Dorchester County.

Cornersville; post village in Dorchester County.

Cornfield; harbor, a small inlet of Potomac River in St. Mary County.

Cornfield; point in St. Mary County, projecting into Potomac River.

Corn Hammock; a small inlet in Assawoman Bay in Worcester County.

Corriganville; post village in Allegany County.

Corsica; river, a small tributary of Chester River in Queen Anne County.

Costen; station in Somerset County on the New York, Philadelphia and Norfolk Railroad.

Cottage Grove; village in Somerset County.

Cotter; cove, a small inlet of Chincoteague Bay in Worcester County.

Cottingham; ferry on Pocomoke River in Worcester County.

Counallor; point in Anne Arundel County, projecting into West River.

Courthouse; point in Cecil County, projecting into Elk River.

Cove; point in Calvert County, projecting into Chesapeake Bay.   A light-house is erected thereon.

Cove; post village in Garrett County.

Cove; run, a small branch of Bear Creek in Garrett County.

Covepoint; post village in Calvert County.

Covey; creek, a small inlet of Trippe Bay in Dorchester County.

Cow; creek, a small tributary of Nanticoke River in Dorchester County.

Cowentown; post village in Cecil County.

Cox; creek, a small stream flowing into Eastern Bay in Queen Anne County.

Cox; creek, a small tributary of West River in Anne Arundel County.

Cox; creek, a small tributary of Patapsco River in Anne Arundel County.

Cox; neck, a strip of land between Cox and Crab Alley creeks in Queen Anne County.

Cox; point in Baltimore County, projecting into Back River.

Cox; post village in Calvert County on the Philadelphia, Baltimore and Washington Railroad.

Crab; point in Dorchester County, projecting into Honga River.

Crab; run, a small tributary of Castleman River in Garrett County.

Crab Alley; creek, a small stream flowing into Eastern Bay in Queen Anne County.

Crab Alley; neck, a strip of land between Crab Alley Creek and Prospect Bay in Queen Anne County.

Crabs; small branch of Rock Creek in Montgomery County.

Crabtree; creek, a small tributary of Savage River in Garrett County.

Craigtown; village in Cecil County.

Crampton; gap in the Blue Ridge Mountains in Frederick County.

Cranberry; run, a small tributary of Patapsco River in Carroll County.

Crane; cove, a small inlet of Big Annemessex Bay in Somerset County.

Crapo; post village in Dorchester County.

Creagerstown; village in Frederick County.

Crellin; post village in Garrett County.

Cremona; creek, a small tributary of Patuxent River in St. Mary County.

Cresaptown; post village in Allegany County.

Creswell; village in Harford County.

Cristfield; town in Somerset County. Population, 3,165.

Crocheron; post village in Dorchester County.

Cromleys Mountain; village in Cecil County.

Cromwell; village in Anne Arundel County.

Cronhardt; post village in Baltimore County.

Cropley; post village in Montgomery County.

Cropper; small, almost entirely marshy island in Newport Bay in Worcester County.

Crooked; run, a small branch of North Branch of Potomac River in Garrett County.

Croom Station; post village in Prince George County on the Philadelphia, Baltimore and Washington Railroad.

Crosby; village in Kent County.

Crosierdoer; creek, a small tributary of Choptank River in Talbot County.

Cross; creek, a small tributary of South River in Anne Arundel County.

Crossroads; post village in Charles County.

Crownsville; post village in Anne Arundel County on the Annapolis, Washington and Baltimore Railroad.

Crumpton; village in Queen Anne County. Population, 207.

Cub Hill; village in Baltimore County.

Cuckold; creek, a small branch of Patuxent River in St. Mary County.

Cuckold; creek, a small branch of Mill Creek in St. Mary County.

Cuckold; creek, a small branch of Potomac River in Charles County.

Cuckold; point in Baltimore County, projecting into Back River.

Cumberland; county seat of Allegany County on the Baltimore and Ohio, the Cumberland and Pennsylvania, the George's Creek and Cumberland, the Pennsylvania, and the West Virginia Central and Pittsburg railroads. Population, 17,128.

Cumberstone; post village in Anne Arundel County.

Cummings; creek, a small branch of Harris Creek in Talbot County.

Curtail; small branch of Monocacy River in Frederick County.

Curtis; creek, a tributary to Curtis Bay in Anne Arundel County.

Curtis; point in Anne Arundel County, projecting into Chesapeake Bay.

Curtis Bay Junction; village in Baltimore County on the Baltimore and Ohio Railroad.

Cutmaptico; creek, a small tributary of Wicomico River in Wicomico County.

Cylburn; village in Baltimore County on Northern Central Railway.

Cypress; branch, a small tributary of Chester River in Kent County.

Dailsville; village in Dorchester County.

Daisy; post village in Howard County.

Dan; run, a small tributary of North Branch of Potomac River in Allegany County.
Daniel; village in Carroll County.
Dans; mountain, a summit of Allegany Front in Allegany County with a maximum altitude of 2,882 feet in Dans Rock, and a rise of over 2,000 feet above the North Branch of Potomac River, which is at its base.
Dans Rock; summit in Dans Mountain in Allegany County. Height, 2,882 feet.
Damascus; town in Montgomery County. Population, 148.
Dames Quarter; creek, a small tributary of Wicomico River in Somerset County.
Dames Quarter; post village in Somerset County.
Dar; post village in Baltimore County.
Dares Wharf; post village in Calvert County.
Dargan; post village in Washington County.
Dark Hollow; run, a small branch of Whitemarsh Run in Baltimore County.
Darlington; village in Harford County. Population, 260.
Darnall; post village in Anne Arundel County.
Darnestown; post village in Montgomery County.
Davidsonville; post village in Anne Arundel County.
Davis; creek, a small tributary of Choptank River in Dorchester County.
Davis; creek, a small branch of Langford Bay in Kent County.
Davis; station in Howard County on the Baltimore and Ohio Railroad.
Davisonville; post village in Montgomery County.
Dawson; post village in Allegany County.
Dawsonville; village in Montgomery County.
Days; point in Harford County, projecting into Gunpowder River.
Daysville; village in Frederick County.
Dayton; post village in Howard County.
Deal; island in Tangier Sound in Somerset County, nearly half of which is sea marsh.
Deale; post village in Anne Arundel County.
Deal Island; post village in Somerset County.
Deep; cove, a small inlet of Chester River in Kent County.
Deep; creek, a small stream flowing through Howard and Baltimore counties into Patapsco River.
Deep; creek, a small stream in St. Mary County flowing into Chesapeake Bay.
Deep; creek, a small tributary of Back River in Baltimore County.
Deep; creek, a small branch of Broad Creek in Harford County.
Deep; creek, a small stream in Anne Arundel County flowing into Chesapeake Bay.
Deep; creek, a small tributary of Magothy River in Anne Arundel County.
Deep; creek, a tributary of Youghiogheny River in Garrett County.
Deep; landing on Patuxent River in Calvert County.
Deep; neck, a strip of land between Edge and Irish creeks in Talbot County.
Deep; point in Charles County, projecting into Potomac River.
Deep; point projecting into Chesapeake Bay in St. Mary County.
Deep; point in Kent County, projecting into Chester River.
Deep; point in Queen Anne County, projecting into Chester River.
Deep; run, a stream on boundary between Howard and Anne Arundel counties, a tributary of Patapsco River.
Deep Banks; small marshy island in Holland Straits in Somerset County.
Deep Neck; point in Talbot County, projecting into Broad Creek.
Deer; creek, a tributary of Susquehanna River rising in Pennsylvania and flowing across the northeast corner of Baltimore County into Harford County.
Deercreek; post village in Harford County.
Deer Park; town in Garrett County on the Baltimore and Ohio Railroad. Population, 203.
Delight; village in Baltimore County.
Delmar; town in Wicomico County. Population, 659.

Dennings; village in Carroll County.

Dennis; creek, a small branch of Quantico Creek in Wicomico County.

Denton; county seat of Caroline County. Population, 900.

Dentsville; post village in Charles County.

Derwood; post village in Montgomery County on the Baltimore and Ohio Railroad.

De Sales; village in Baltimore County.

Detmold; hill on boundary between Garrett and Allegany counties.

Devil; small marshy island in Assawoman Bay in Worcester County.

Devil Nest; creek, a small tributary of Zekiah Swamp in Charles County.

Dick; branch, a small tributary of Little Gunpowder Falls in Baltimore County.

Dickens; post village in Allegany County.

Dickerson; post village in Montgomery County on the Baltimore and Ohio Railroad.

Ditch; run, a small tributary of Potomac River in Washington County.

Dividing; creek, a tributary of Pocomoke River on boundary between Somerset and Worcester counties.

Dobbin; two small islands in Magothy River in Anne Arundel County.

Dodson; post village in Garrett County.

Dog; mountain ridge in Garrett County.

Dog and Bitch; small marshy island in Isle of Wight Bay in Worcester County.

Dogwood; small branch of Little Elk River in Cecil County.

Dogwood; small tributary of Patapsco River in Baltimore County.

Dominion; village in Queen Anne County.

Doncaster; post village in Charles County.

Dorchester; county, organized in 1669: extends from Chesapeake Bay to the Delaware state line, and is bounded on the southeast by Nanticoke River and on the north by Choptank River. The surface is generally level, although the upper part of the county undulates considerably. The area is 608 square miles, of which more than a third, or 128,160 acres, was under cultivation in 1900. The population for the same year was 27,962. The county seat is Cambridge, a town of about 5,000 inhabitants, while the next town in size is East Newmarket, which had a population of 1,267 in 1900. The average magnetic declination in the county in 1900 was 5° 35′ west. The annual rainfall commonly ranges between 45 and 50 inches, and the mean annual temperature between 55° and 60°.

Dorsey; post village in Howard County on the Baltimore and Ohio Railroad.

Dorseys; run, a small tributary of Little Patuxent River in Howard and Anne Arundel counties.

Dorseys; run, a small tributary of Patapsco River in Howard County.

Dorseys Run; station in Howard County on the Baltimore and Ohio Railroad.

Double Bridge; branch, a small tributary of Pocomoke River in Worcester County.

Double Lick; run, a small branch of Blackhawk Run in Garrett County.

Double Pipecreek; post village in Carroll County on the Western Maryland Railroad.

Doubs; post village in Frederick County on the Baltimore and Ohio Railroad.

Douglass; run, a small branch of Cherry Run in Garrett County.

Dougherty; creek, a small tributary of Big Annemessex River in Somerset County.

Doughoregan; post village in Howard County.

Downes; post village in Caroline County on the Queen Anne's Railroad.

Downesville; post village in Washington County.

Dove; cove, a small inlet of Bush River in Harford County.

Drawbridge; post village in Dorchester County.

Drayden; post village in St. Mary County.

Druid; lake, in Druid Hill Park, a suburb of Baltimore City within its chartered limits.

Druid Hill Park; principal park of Baltimore City.
Drum; point in Baltimore County, projecting into Back River.
Drum; point in Calvert County, projecting into Patuxent River.
Drum; point in Somerset County, projecting into Manokin River.
Drum; point in Somerset County, projecting into Tangier Sound.
Drum; point in Worcester County, projecting into Assawoman Bay.
Drum; point in Worcester County, projecting into Isle of Wight Bay.
Drumcliff; post village in St. Mary County.
Drum Point; cove, a small inlet of Manokin River in Somerset County.
Drum Point; village in Calvert County.
Drunkard Lick; run, a small tributary of Youghiogheny River in Garrett County.
Drury; post village in Anne Arundel County.
Dry; run, a small tributary of Savage River in Garrett County.
Drybranch; village in Harford County.
Dry Seneca; creek, a small branch of Seneca Creek in Montgomery County.
Dublin; post village in Harford County.
Dublin; village in Somerset County.
Dubois; post village in Charles County.
Duck Point; cove, a small inlet of Honga River in Dorchester County.
Duffield; village in Charles County.
Duffy; creek, a small tributary of Sassafras River in Cecil County.
Dulaney; creek, a small tributary of Gunpowder Falls in Baltimore County.
Dulaney Valley; post village in Baltimore County.
Duley; post village in Prince George County.
Dun; cove, a small inlet of Harris Creek in Talbot County.
Dung; creek, a small tributary of Nanticoke River in Wicomico County.
Dunghill; summit in Negro Mountain in Garrett County.
Dunkirk; post village in Calvert County.
Dunnock; island, a bit of elevated dry land in the sea marshes of Dorchester County.
Durden; creek, a small tributary of Chester River in Kent County.
Dutch; small island in Susquehanna River in Harford County.
Duvall; creek, a small tributary of Whitehall River in Anne Arundel County.
Duvall; creek, a small tributary of South River in Anne Arundel County.
Dynard; post village in St. Mary County.
Eagle; hill in Anne Arundel County.
Eagle; small marshy island in St. Martin River in Worcester County.
Eagle; rock, a summit in Backbone Mountain in Garrett County. Height, 3,162 feet.
Eakles Mills; post village in Washington County on the Baltimore and Ohio Railroad.
Eakton Mills; village in Frederick County.
Earleigh Heights; post village in Anne Arundel County on the Baltimore and Annapolis Short Line Railroad.
Earlton; post village in Harford County.
Earlville; post village in Cecil County.
East; branch, a small tributary of Little Elk River in Cecil County.
East; small branch of Winters Creek in Harford County.
East; creek, a small tributary of Pocomoke River in Somerset County
East; run, a small tributary of St. Mary River in St. Mary County.
Eastern; bay, an arm of Chesapeake Bay on boundary between Queen Anne and Talbot counties.
Eastern; neck, a strip of land between Chesapeake Bay and Chester River in Kent County.
Eastern Neck; small island at mouth of Chester River in Kent County.

East New Market; town in Dorchester County. Population, 1,267.

Easton; county seat of Talbot County, on the Baltimore, Chesapeake and Atlantic and the Philadelphia, Baltimore and Washington railroads. Population, 3,074.

Easton; point in Talbot County, projecting into Tred Avon River.

Eastport; post village in Anne Arundel County.

Eber; village in Cecil County.

Eckhart Mines; post village in Allegany County.

Eden; post village in Somerset County on the New York, Philadelphia and Norfolk Railroad.

Edesville; post village in Kent County.

Edge; creek, a small branch of Broad Creek, in Talbot County.

Edgemont; post village in Washington County on the Western Maryland Railroad.

Edgewater; post village in Anne Arundel County.

Edgewood; post village in Harford County on the Philadelphia, Baltimore and Washington Railroad.

Ednor; post village in Montgomery County.

Edwards Ferry; post village in Montgomery County.

Edwin; post village in Somerset County.

Egg; hill in Cecil County. Height, 442 feet.

Eklo; village in Baltimore County.

Elbow; small branch of Deer Creek in Harford County.

Elbow; hill in bend of Savage River in Garrett County.

Elbow; mountain, between Savage River and Big Savage River in Garrett County.

Elbow; ridge, small mountain ridge in Washington County.

Elder; post village in Garrett County.

Eldersburg; village in Carroll County.

Elioak; post village in Howard County.

Elk; neck, between Elk and Northeast rivers in Cecil County.

Elk; river in Cecil County tributary to Chesapeake Bay.

Elklick; run, a small branch of Georges Creek in Allegany County.

Elk Lick; run, a small tributary of Savage River in Garrett County.

Elkneck; post village in Cecil County.

Elkridge; village in Howard County on Baltimore and Ohio Railroad.

Elkton; county seat of Cecil County on the Philadelphia, Baltimore and Washington Railroad. Population, 2,542.

Elkton; landing on Elk River in Cecil County.

Ellerslie; post village and station in Allegany County on the Baltimore and Ohio Railroad.

Ellicott; county seat of Howard County on the Baltimore and Ohio Railroad. Population, 1,331.

Elliott; island, a tract of elevated dry land in sea marshes of Dorchester County.

Elliott; post village in Dorchester County on Elliott Island.

Ellis; bay, an inlet at mouth of Wicomico River in Wicomico County, into which flows Broad Creek.

Ellwood; post village in Dorchester County.

Elmer; post village in Montgomery County.

Elsio; post village in Baltimore County.

Elvaton; post village in Anne Arundel County on the Baltimore and Annapolis Short Line Railroad.

Emmitsburg; town in Frederick County on the Emmitsburg Railroad. Population, 849.

Emmorton; post village in Harford County.

Emory; cove, a small inlet of Corsica River in Queen Anne County.

Emory; post village in St. Mary County.

Emory Grove; post village in Baltimore County on the Western Maryland Railroad.

Engle Mills; post village in Garrett County.

Ernstville; village in Washington County.

Etchison; post village in Montgomery County.

Evans; hill in Garrett County.

Evitts; creek, a small branch of North Branch of Potomac River in Allegany County.

Evitts; mountain, a small mountain ridge in Allegany County.

Evna; village in Baltimore County.

Ewell; post village in Somerset County.

Exline; village in Washington County.

Fairbank; post village in Talbot County.

Fairhaven; post village in Anne Arundel County.

Fairhill; post village in Cecil County.

Fairland; post village in Montgomery County.

Fairlee; creek, a small stream in Kent County flowing into Chesapeake Bay.

Fairlee; post village in Kent County.

Fairmont; post village in Somerset County.

Fair Sweep; village in Garrett County.

Fairview; point in Harford County, projecting into Bush River.

Fairview; post village in Washington County on the Western Maryland Railroad.

Fairview; village in Talbot County.

Falling; small branch of Deer Creek in Harford County.

Fallston; post village in Harford County on the Maryland and Pennsylvania Railroad.

Far; creek, a small tributary of Honga River in Dorchester County.

Farhole; creek, a small tributary of Tred Avon River in Talbot County.

Farm; creek, a small stream in Dorchester County flowing into Fishing Bay.

Farmington; landing on Piscataway Creek in Prince George County.

Farmington; post village in Cecil County.

Fassett; point in Dorchester County, projecting into Sinepuxent Bay.

Faulkner; post village in Charles County.

Fearer; post village in Garrett County.

Federal; hill in Allegany County. Height, 2,106 feet.

Federal Hill; village in Harford County.

Federalsburg; village in Caroline County on the Philadelphia, Baltimore and Washington Railroad. Population, 539.

Federal Spring; small branch of Western Branch in Prince George County.

Feik; run, a small branch of Bear Creek in Garrett County.

Fenwick; creek, a small tributary of Wicomico River in Charles county.

Ferry; landing on Patuxent River in Prince George County.

Ferry; neck, a strip of land between Tred Avon River and Broad Creek in Talbot County.

Ferry; point in Baltimore County, projecting into Patapsco River.

Ferry; point in Anne Arundel County, projecting into Curtis Bay.

Ferry; point of Anne Arundel County, projecting into South River.

Fifteenmile; creek, a tributary of Potomac River in Allegany County.

Finksburg; post village in Carroll County on the Western Maryland Railroad.

Finzel; post village in Garrett County.

First Mine; branch, a small tributary of Gunpowder Falls in Baltimore County.

Fishing; bay, an arm of Chesapeake Bay in Dorchester County.

Fishing; creek, a small stream flowing into Chesapeake Bay in Calvert County.

Fishing; creek, a small tributary of Honga River in Dorchester County.

Fishing; creek, a small tributary of Manokin River in Somerset County.
Fishing; island, a bit of elevated dry land in sea marshes of Somerset County.
Fishing; point in Somerset County, projecting into Manokin River.
Fishing; point in Anne Arundel County, projecting into Curtis Bay.
Fishing; point, the western extremity of Elliott Island in Dorchester County, projecting into Fishing Bay.
Fishing; point in St. Mary County, projecting into Patuxent River.
Fishing; point on Smith Island in Somerset County, projecting into Chesapeake Bay.
Fishing Creek; post village in Dorchester County.
Five Forks; village in Baltimore County.
Five Points; village in Wicomico County.
Flat; creek, a small branch of Middle Creek in Frederick County.
Flatcap; point in Somerset County, projecting into Big Annemessex River.
Flatland; cove, a small inlet near mouth of Big Annemessex River in Somerset County.
Flintstone; post village in Allegany County.
Flintville; post village in Harford County.
Flood; creek, a small branch of Potomac River in St. Mary County.
Florence; post village in Howard County.
Fog; point on Smith Island in Somerset County, projecting into Chesapeake Bay.
Fog Point; cove, a small inlet of Hedge Straits on Smith Island in Somerset County.
Folly; small branch of Western Branch in Prince George County.
Folly; run, a small tributary of North Branch of Potomac River in Garrett County.
Fooks; pond in Wicomico County drained by Tonytank Creek, a tributary of Wicomico River.
Fooks School; village in Wicomico County.
Ford; point in Harford County, projecting into Chesapeake Bay.
Fords; landing on Elk River in Cecil County.
Fords; wharf on Muddy Creek in Somerset County.
Ford Store; post village in Queen Anne County.
Foreman; landing on Wye River in Queen Anne County.
Forest Glen; post village in Montgomery County on the Baltimore and Ohio Railroad.
Foresthill; post village in Harford County.
Forestville; village in Prince George County.
Fork; creek, a small tributary of Savage River in Garrett County.
Fork; post village in Baltimore County.
Fork of Owens; creek, a small tributary of Monocacy River in Frederick County.
Formans; branch, a small tributary of Chester River in Queen Anne County.
Fort; hill, in Allegany County. Height, 1,621 feet.
Fort; point in St. Mary County, projecting into St. Mary River.
Fort Foote; fort in Prince George County on Potomac River.
Fort Frederick; fort in Washington County.
Fort McHenry; fort on Patapsco River within chartered limits of Baltimore city.
Fort Pendleton; fort in Garrett County.
Fort Republic; village in Calvert County.
Fort Washington; post village in Prince George County on Potomac River.
Foster; branch, a small tributary of Bush River in Harford County.
Fountain Green; post village in Harford County.
Fourmile; mountain ridge separating Muddick Run and Savage River in Garrett County.

Fourth Mine; branch, a small tributary of Gunpowder Falls in Baltimore County.

Fowblesburg; post village in Baltimore County on the Western Maryland Railroad.

Fowling; creek, a small tributary of Choptank River in Caroline County.

Fowling Creek; post village in Caroline County.

Fox; run, a small branch of Cherry Run in Garrett County.

Foys; hill in Cecil County. Height, 300 feet.

Frankford; village in Wicomico County.

Franklin; branch, a small tributary of Pocomoke River in Worcester County.

Franklin; point in Anne Arundel County, projecting into Chesapeake Bay.

Franklin; village in Allegany County on the Cumberland and Pennsylvania Railroad.

Franklin; village in Baltimore County.

Franklinville; post village in Baltimore County.

Frazier; post village in Calvert County.

Frederick; city, county seat of Frederick County on the Baltimore and Ohio Railroad. Population, 9,296.

Frederick; county, bounded on the north by Pennsylvania, on the east by Carroll County, southeast by Montgomery County, west by Blue Ridge Mountains, and south by Potomac River. The surface is undulating, partly mountainous; the Catoctin Mountains dividing the county into two broad valleys, that to the westward being drained by Catoctin River and its branches and the one eastward by Monocacy River, both rivers flowing into Potomac River. The area of the county is 662 square miles, nearly three-fourths of which, or 308,041 acres, being under cultivation in 1900. The population for the same year was 51,920. The county seat and principal city is Frederick, a town of about 9,300 inhabitants. It also contains Brunswick, a town of about 2,500 inhabitants. The average magnectic declination in the county in 1900 was 5° 10′ west. The annual rainfall commonly ranges between 45 and 50 inches and the mean annual temperature between 50° and 55°.

Frederick Junction; station in Frederick County on the Baltimore and Ohio Railroad.

Fredericktown; village in Cecil County.

Freedom; village in Carroll County.

Freeland; post village in Baltimore County on the Northern Central Railway.

Freeman; creek, a small tributary of Sassafras River in Kent County.

Freetown; village in Somerset County.

Frenchtown; village in Cecil County on the Philadelphia, Baltimore and Washington Railroad.

Friendly; post village in Prince George County.

Friendship; post village in Anne Arundel County.

Friendship; suburb of Baltimore City within its chartered limits.

Friendship; village in St. Mary County.

Friendship; station in Worcester County on the Philadelphia, Baltimore and Washington Railroad.

Friendsville; post village in Garrett County on the Baltimore and Ohio Railroad.

Frog; hollow in Collier Mountain in Allegany County.

Frog; point in Dorchester County, projecting into Nanticoke River.

Frogeye; village in Somerset County.

Frogtown; village in Harford County.

Front Wye; river on boundary between Queen Anne and Talbot counties, a tributary of Wye River.

Frost; village in Anne Arundel County.

Frostburg; town in Allegany County on the Cumberland and Pennsylvania Railroad. Population, 5,274.

Frosts; village in Allegany County on the West Virginia Central and Pittsburg Railroad.

Frozen Camp; run, a small branch of Cherry Run in Garrett County.

Fruitland; post village in Wicomico County on the New York, Philadelphia and Norfolk Railroad.

Fryers; wharf on Sassafras River in Kent County.

Fryingpan; cove, a small inlet of Chester River in Kent County.

Fulford; post village in Harford County.

Fullerton, post village in Baltimore County.

Fulton; post village in Howard County.

Funkstown; town in Washington County. Population, 559.

Furnace; creek, a small tributary of Chesapeake Bay.

Furnace; creek, a small branch of Curtis Creek in Anne Arundel County.

Furnace; creek, a small tributary of Potomac River in Frederick County.

Furnace; village in Harford County.

Furnace; village in Worcester County.

Gab; small island at mouth of Lighting Knot Cove in Somerset County.

Gaither; post village in Carroll County.

Gaithersburg; town in Montgomery County on the Baltimore and Ohio Railroad. Population, 547.

Galena; town in Kent County. Population, 251.

Gales; creek, a small branch of Rhode River in Anne Arundel County.

Gales; creek, a small tributary of Big Annemessex River in Somerset County.

Gales; wharf on Worton Creek in Kent County.

Galestown; post village in Dorchester County.

Gallant Green; post village in Charles County on the Washington, Potomac and Chesapeake Railroad.

Galloway; creek, a small branch of Middle Creek in Baltimore County.

Galloway; point in Baltimore County, projecting into Middle River.

Galloways; post village in Anne Arundel County.

Gambage; small marshy island in Turville Creek in Worcester County.

Gamber; village in Carroll County.

Gambrills; post village on the Annapolis, Washington and Batimore Railroad.

Gapland; post village in Washington County on the Baltimore and Ohio Railroad.

Garland; post village in Harford County.

Garrett; county, bounded on the north by Pennsylvania, on the east by Washington County, on the south by the North Branch of Potomac River, and on the west by West Virginia. The county is comprised mainly in the Allegany Plateau, having an undulating surface with an average altitude not far from 2,500 feet, and rising to a mountain range above the North Branch of Potomac River, known as Backbone Mountain, which has an extreme height of 3,400 feet and an average altitude of 3,000 feet. The northwest part is drained by Youghiogheny River to the Ohio and the southeast part by North Branch of the Potomac. The area is 240 square miles, of which less than 30 per cent, or 123,932 acres, was under cultivation in 1900. The population for the same year was 17,701. The county seat is Oakland, with a population of 2,170 in 1900. The average magnetic declination in the county in 1900 was 3° 45′. The annual rainfall commonly ranges between 45 and 50 inches, and the mean annual temperature between 45° and 50°.

Garrett; small island in Susquehanna River in Cecil County.

Garrett Park; town in Montgomery County on the Baltimore and Ohio Railroad. Population, 175.

Garrison; post village in Baltimore County.

Gary; post village in Howard County.

Gasheys; creek, a small branch of Swan Creek in Harford County.

Geanquakin; creek, a small tributary of Manokin River in Somerset County.

Gem Mills; village in Baltimore County.

Gentsville; village in Baltimore County.

George; hill in Garrett County. Height, 3,004 feet.

Georges; creek, a tributary of North Branch of Potomac River on boundary between Allegany and Garrett counties.

Georges; creek, a small tributary of Gunpowder Falls in Baltimore County.

Georges Island; landing in Worcester County on Chincoteague Bay.

Georgetown; post village in Kent County.

German; creek, a small branch of Tuckahoe Creek in Queen Anne County.

Germantown; post village in Montgomery County on the Baltimore and Ohio Railroad.

Gibson; small island in Chesapeake Bay in Anne Arundel County.

Gibson; village in Harford County.

Gilbert; run, a small stream in Charles County tributary to Gilbert Swamp.

Gilbert; swamp, a small marshy stream flowing into Wicomico River in Charles County.

Gillens Falls; small branch of South Branch of Patapsco River in Carroll County.

Gilmore; post village in Allegany County.

Gilpen; post village in Allegany County.

Ginrichs; station in Baltimore County on the Western Maryland Railroad.

Girdletree; town in Worcester County on the Philadelphia, Baltimore and Washington Railroad. Population, 336.

Gise; village in Garret County.

Gist; village in Kent County.

Gittings; post village in Baltimore County.

Givens; branch, a small stream draining Adkins Pond and flowing into Pocomoke River in Wicomico County.

Glade; run, a small tributary of North Branch of Potomac River in Garrett County.

Gladstone; branch, a small tributary of Nanticoke River in Dorchester County.

Glebe; creek, a small tributary of Miles River in Talbot County.

Glebe; creek, a small branch of South River in Anne Arundel County.

Glen; post village in Montgomery County.

Glenarm; post village in Baltimore County on the Maryland and Pennsylvania Railroad.

Glenburnie; station in Anne Arundel County on the Baltimore and Annapolis Short Line Railroad.

Glencoe; post village in Baltimore County on the Northern Central Railway.

Glen Cove; village in Harford County.

Glen Echo; post village in Montgomery County.

Glenelg; post village in Howard County.

Glen Falls; station in Baltimore County on the Western Maryland Railroad.

Glen Morris; post village in Baltimore County on the Western Maryland Railroad.

Glenndale; post village in Prince George County on the Philadelphia, Baltimore and Washington Railroad.

Glenville: post village in Harford County.

Glenwood; post village in Howard County.

Glymont; post village in Charles County.

Glyndon; post village in Baltimore County on the Western Maryland Railroad.

Gods Grace; point in Calvert County, projecting into Patuxent River.

Goldenhill; post village in Dorchester County.

Golden Ring; station in Baltimore County on the Baltimore and Ohio Railroad.

Goldsboro; creek, a small tributary of Tred Avon River in Talbot County.

Goldsboro; post village in Caroline County.

Golts; post village and station in Kent County on the Philadelphia, Baltimore and Washington Railroad.

Good Luck; village in Prince George County.

Goodwill; village in Worcester County.

Goody Hill; small branch of Basset Creek in Worcester County.

Goose; creek, a small stream in Somerset County flowing into Kedge Strait.

Goose; creek, a small tributary of Manokin River in Somerset County.

Goose; creek, a small stream in Dorchester County flowing into Fishing Bay.

Goose; creek, a small tributary of Choptank River in Dorchester County.

Goose; point in Worcester County, projecting into Sinepuxent Bay.

Goose; pond forming a small inlet of Assawoman Bay in Worcester County.

Goose; pond in Anne Arundel County having outlet into Chesapeake Bay.

Gordon; point in Queen Anne County, projecting into Chester River.

Gorman; village in Garrett County.

Gorsuch; post village in Carroll County on the Baltimore and Ohio Railroad.

Gorsuch Mills; village in Baltimore County.

Gortner; post village in Garrett County.

Goshen; creek, a small tributary of Great Seneca Creek in Montgomery County.

Goshen; post village in Montgomery County.

Governor Run; post village in Calvert County.

Grace; creek, a small branch of Broad Creek in Talbot County.

Grace; point in Baltimore County, projecting into Bush River.

Graceham; post village in Frederick County on the Western Maryland Railroad.

Grafton; village in Charles County.

Grafton Shops; village in Harford County.

Graney; creek, a small tributary to Chesapeake Bay in Queen Anne County.

Grange; post village in Baltimore County on the Philadelphia, Baltimore and Washington Railroad.

Granite; post village in Baltimore County.

Grantsville; town in Garrett County. Population, 175.

Grassy; small marshy island in Isle of Wight Bay in Worcester County.

Gratitude; post village in Kent County.

Gravelly; point in Dorchester County, projecting into Nanticoke River.

Graveyard; creek, a small branch of Deer Creek in Harford County.

Graveyard; creek, a small tributary of Severn River in Anne Arundel County.

Gray; point in St. Mary County, projecting into Potomac River.

Grays; hill in Cecil County. Height, 268 feet.

Grays; island, a bit of elevated dry land in sea marshes of Dorchester County.

Grays Corner; village in Worcester County.

Grays Inn; creek, a small tributary of Chester River in Kent County.

Grayton; post village in Charles County.

Great; bay, a small inlet of Tar Bay in Dorchester County.

Great; cove, a small inlet of Tangier Sound in Dorchester County.

Great; falls in the Potomac River between Fairfax County, Va., and Montgomery County.

Great Bohemia; creek, rises in Delaware and flows through Cecil County into Bohemia River.

Great Egging; beach, on sand bar separating Sinepuxent Bay from the Atlantic Ocean in Worcester County.

Greatfalls; post village in Montgomery County.

Great Marsh; point in Talbot County, projecting into Chesapeake Bay.

Great Mills; post village in St. Mary County.

Great Seneca; creek, a tributary of Potomac River in Montgomery County.

Great Tonoloway; creek, a small branch of Potomac River in Washington County.

Green; point in Worcester County, projecting into Sinepuxent Bay.

Green; run, a small tributary of Pocomoke River in Wicomico County.

Green; mountain ridge separating Town Creek from Purstane Run in Allegany County.

Greenbury; point in Anne Arundel County, projecting into Annapolis Roads.

Greenbush; point in Cecil County, projecting into Elk River.

Greenfield Mills; village in Frederick County.

Green Glade; run, a small branch of Deep Creek in Garrett County.

Greenhill; village in Somerset County.

Greenhurst; post village in Cecil County.

Green Marsh; point in Baltimore County, projecting into Back River.

Greenmound; post village in Carroll County on the Western Maryland Railroad.

Greenock; post village in Anne Arundel County.

Green Point; wharf in Kent County on Worton Creek.

Greens; branch, a small tributary of Gunpowder Falls in Baltimore County.

Greensboro; town in Caroline County on the Philadelphia, Baltimore and Washington Railroad. Population, 641.

Green Spring; village in Baltimore County.

Green Spring Junction; station in Baltimore County on the Northern Central and Western Maryland railroads.

Green Valley; village in Frederick County.

Greenwood; creek, a small stream in Queen Anne County flowing into Eastern Bay.

Greenwood; post village in Baltimore County on the Western Maryland Railroad.

Greys; creek, a small stream in Worcester County flowing into Assawoman Bay.

Greys; small inlet of Newport Bay in Worcester County.

Greystone; village in Baltimore County.

Griffin; post village in Caroline County.

Grifton; post village in Montgomery County.

Grimes; creek, a small tributary of Nanticoke River in Wicomico County.

Grimes; post village in Washington County on the Norfolk and Western Railway.

Grove; small tributary of Chester River in Queen Anne County.

Grove; neck, a strip of land between Sassafras River and Pond Creek in Cecil County.

Grove; point in Cecil County, projecting into mouth of Sassafras River.

Grove; post village in Caroline County on the Norfolk and Western Railway.

Guard; post village in Garrett County.

Guest; point in St. Mary County, projecting into St. Clement Bay.

Guilford; post village in Hóward County.

Gum; point in Kent County, projecting into Chester River.

Gumbridge; branch, a small tributary of Pocomoke River in Worcester County.

Gum Swamp; village in Dorchester County.

Gunby; creek, a small tributary to Pocomoke Sound in Somerset County.

Gunner; creek, a small branch of Great Seneca Creek in Montgomery County.

Gunpowder; neck, a strip of land between Gunpowder and Bush rivers in Harford County.

Gunpowder; river, a large estuary on boundary between Harford and Baltimore counties flowing into Chesapeake Bay.

Gunpowder Falls; river, a tributary of Gunpowder River in Baltimore County.

Guys; village in Queen Anne County.

Gwynnbrook; post village in Baltimore County.

Gwynns Falls; creek in Baltimore County near Baltimore; flows into Middle Branch of Patapsco River.

Habnab; post village in Somerset County.

Hackett; point in Anne Arundel County, projecting into Annapolis Roads.

Hagerstown; county seat of Washington County on the Baltimore and Ohio, the Cumberland Valley, the Norfolk and Western, and the Western Maryland railroads. Population, 13,591.

Haha; small branch of Otter Point Creek in Harford County.

Haight; village in Carroll County.

Hail; creek, a small tributary of Chester River in Kent County.

Hail; point in Kent County, projecting into Chester River.

Haines; point in Somerset County, projecting into Tangier Sound.

Halethorp; post village in Baltimore County on the Baltimore and Ohio and the Philadelphia, Baltimore and Washington railroads.

Halfway; post village in Washington County on the Cumberland Valley Railroad.

Hall; creek, a small tributary of Patuxent River in Calvert County.

Hall; creek, a small stream in Somerset County flowing into Big Annemessex River.

Hall; point in Somerset County, projecting into Tangier Sound.

Hall; village in Prince George County on the Philadelphia, Baltimore and Washington Railroad.

Hallowing; point in Calvert County, projecting into Patuxent River.

Halls; hill, a summit in Hoop Pole Mountain Ridge in Garrett County. Height, 2,700 feet.

Halls; post village in Prince George County.

Halpine; station in Montgomery County on the Baltimore and Ohio Railroad.

Hambleton; creek, a small tributary of Chester River in Queen Anne County.

Hambleton; creek, a small branch of Miles Creek in Talbot County.

Hambleton; small island in Broad Creek in Talbot County.

Hambleton; post village in Talbot County.

Hambrook; sand bar in Choptank River in Dorchester County.

Hamburg; village in Frederick County.

Hammock; point in Somerset County, projecting into Little Annemessex River.

Hammond; branch, a tributary of Little Patuxent River in Howard County.

Hampden; suburb of Baltimore city within its chartered limits.

Hampstead; post village in Carroll County on the Western Maryland Railroad.

Hance; point in Cecil County, projecting into Northeast River.

Hancock; run, a small branch of Nanjemoy Creek in Charles County.

Hancock; town in Wahington County; population, 824.

Handys; hammock, a bit of marsh in Newport Bay in Worcester County.

Hanesville; post village in Kent County.

Hanover; post village in Howard County on Baltimore and Ohio Railroad.

Hansonville; village in Frederick County.

Happy Valley; branch, a small tributary of Susquehanna River in Cecil County.

Harbor; cove, a small inlet of Eastern Bay in Talbot County.

Hardesty; post village in Prince George County.

Hardship; branch, a small tributary of Pocomoke River in Worcester County.

Hardys Hole; passage between Mills Island and a small adjacent island in Chincoteague Bay in Worcester County.

Harford; county, organized in 1773, is bounded on the east and southeast by Susquehanna River and Chesapeake Bay, north by Pennsylvania, and on the west and southwest by Baltimore County. The surface is varied—the lower part being level, while above the Philadelphia turnpike it is undulating and quite hilly in some parts. It is well drained by the branches of the Little Gunpowder Falls in the lower part, while Deer Creek and its branches drain the northern part. The area is 388 square miles, of which almost three-fourths, or 174,255 acres, was under cultivation in 1900. The population for the same year was 28,269. The county seat is Belair. The average magnetic declination in the county in 1900 was 5° 40′ west. The annual rainfall commonly ranges between 45 and 50 inches, and the mean annual temperature between 50° and 55°.

Harford Furnace; post village in Harford County.

Harkin; village in Harford County.

Harmans; post village and station in Anne Arundel County on the Annapolis, Washington and Baltimore Railroad.

Harmony Grove; post village and station in Frederick County on the Northern Central Railroad.

Harper; creek, a small tributary of Patuxent River in St. Mary County.

Harper; station in Talbot County on the Baltimore, Chesapeake and Atlantic Railway.

Harris; creek, a tributary of Choptank River in Talbot County.

Harris; wharf on Chesapeake Bay in Kent County.

Harris Lot; post village in Charles County.

Harrisonville; village in Baltimore County.

Harrisville; village in Cecil County.

Harry; creek, a small tributary of St. Martin River in Worcester County.

Harry James; creek, a small tributary of Potomac River in St. Mary County.

Hart; small, almost entirely marshy island in Chesepcake Bay in Baltimore County.

Hartley; post village in Baltimore County.

Harvey; village in Washington County.

Harwood; post village in Anne Arundel County on the Baltimore and Ohio Railroad.

Hasty; point in Worcester County, projecting into St. Martin River.

Hathaway; small island in Patapsco River in Baltimore County.

Hauser; post village in Garrett County.

Havemyer Park; village in Prince George County.

Havre de Grace; post village in Harford County on the Baltimore and Ohio and the Philadelphia, Baltimore and Washington railroads.

Hawk; cove, a small inlet of Chesapeake Bay in Baltimore County.

Hawkins; point in Anne Arundel County, projecting into Patapsco River. A lighthouse is erected thereon.

Hawlings; river, a tributary of Patuxent River in Montgomery County.

Hawthorn; cove, a small inlet of Seneca Creek in Baltimore County.

Hayden; post village in Queen Anne County.

Haystack; small branch of Long Green Creek in Baltimore County.

Haystack; pond, a small inlet at mouth of St. Martin River in Worcester County.

Hazard; cove, a small inlet near mouth of Big Annemessex River in Somerset County.

Hazard; point in Somerset County, projecting into mouth of Manokin River.

Hazelnut; small branch of Bens Branch in Frederick County.

Hazen; post village in Allegany County.

Head of Creek; village in Somerset County.

Hearns; village in Wicomico County.

Hebbville; village in Baltimore County.

Hebron; post village in Wicomico County on the Baltimore, Chesapeake and Atlantic Railway.

Helen; post village in St. Mary County.

Hellen; creek, a small tributary of Patuxent River in Calvert County.

Hellen; gut, a small branch of Patuxent River in Calvert County.

Hellen; village in Calvert County.

Hen and Chickens; small marshy island in St. Martin River in Worcester County.

Henderson; post village in Caroline County on the Philadelphia, Baltimore and Washington Railroad.

Henryton; post village in Carroll County on the Baltimore and Ohio Railroad.

Henson; creek, a small tributary of Potomac River in Prince George County.

Hepbron; station in Kent County on the Baltimore, Chesapeake and Atlantic Railway.

Hereford; village in Baltimore County.

Hermanville; post village in St. Mary County.

Hernwood; village in Baltimore County.

Heron; small island in Potomac River in St. Mary County.

Herring; bay, and arm of Chesapeake Bay in Anne Arundel County.

Herring; creek, a small tributary of Herring Bay in Anne Arundel County.

Herring; creek, a small tributary of Choptank River in Caroline County.

Herring; creek, a small tributary of Potomac River in St. Mary County.

Herring; run, a small tributary of Back River in Baltimore County.

Herrington; creek, a tributary of Youghiogheny River in Garrett County.

Hess; post village in Harford County.

Hickory; cove, a small inlet of Honga River in Dorchester County.

Hickory; village in Harford County.

Hickorynut; small island in Susquehanna River in Harford County.

Hicks Mill; village in Prince George County.

Higgin; point in St. Mary County, projecting into Potomac River.

High; point in Cecil County, projecting into Chesapeake Bay.

High; rock, a summit in Big Savage Mountain in Garrett County.   Height, 3,000 feet.

Highfield; post village in Washington County.

Highland; post village in Howard County on the Maryland and Pennsylvania Railroad.

High Point; village in Harford County.

Hill; small marshy island in Assawoman Bay in Worchester County.

Hill; point in Anne Arundel County, projecting into South River.

Hill; run, a small branch of Georges Creek in Allegany County.

Hill; station in Prince George County on the Philadelphia, Baltimore and Washington Railroad.

Hills; point in Dorchester County, projecting into Chesapeake Bay.

Hillsboro; town in Caroline County on the Philadelphia, Baltimore and Washington Railroad.   Population, 196.

Hills Point; cove, a small inlet at mouth of Little Choptank River in Dorchester County.

Hillspoint; post village in Dorchester County.

Hilltop; post village in Charles County.

Hillville; village in St. Mary County.

Hilton; village in Howard County.

Hobbs; post village in Caroline County.

Hoffman; village in Allegany County on the Gunpowder Valley Railroad.

Hog; cove, a small inlet of Honga River in Dorchester County.

Hog; hills in Cecil County.   Height, 300 feet.

Hog; marsh, a swamp in Dorchester County.

Hog; small island in Chesapeake Bay in Calvert County.

Hog; small marshy island south of Marsh Creek in Queen Anne County.

Hoghole; creek, a small stream tributary to Prospect Bay in Queen Anne County.

Hog Island; point in Worcester County, projecting into Chincoteague Bay.

Holland; creek, a small branch of Trappe Creek in Worcester County.

Holland; small, almost entirely marshy island in Holland Straits in Dorchester County.

Holland, point in Anne Arundel County, projecting into Chesapeake Bay.

Holland; point in Somerset County, projecting into Big Annemessex River.

Holland; strait, a passage between Bloodsworth Island and South Marsh on boundary between Dorchester and Somerset counties.

Holland Island; bar, a small island at entrance to Holland Straits in Dorchester County. A light-house is erected thereon.

Holland Island; post village in Dorchester County.

Hollands; small branch of Deer Creek in Harford County.

Hollin Cliff; point in Calvert County, projecting into Patuxent River.

Hollins; station in Baltimore County on the Northern Central Railway.

Hollofield; station in Howard County on the Baltimore and Ohio Railroad.

Hollygrove; station in Worcester County on the Baltimore, Chesapeake and Atlantic Railway.

Hollywood; post village in St. Mary County.

Holton; point in Queen Anne County, projecting into Chester River.

Homeland; station in Baltimore County on the Maryland and Pennsylvania Railroad.

Honga; river, a long winding bay, an arm of Chesapeake Bay.

Hood; point in Queen Anne County, projecting into Prospect Bay.

Hoods Mills; post village in Carroll County on the Baltimore and Ohio Railroad.

Hooper; islands, a long narrow strip of almost entirely marshy land between Honga River and Chesapeake Bay in Dorchester County.

Hooper; neck, a strip of land between Davis and Slaughter creeks in Dorchester County.

Hooper; point in Dorchester County, projecting into Little Choptank River.

Hoopersville; post village in Dorchester County.

Hoop Pole; small mountain ridge in Garrett County.

Hope; post village in Queen Anne County.

Hopewell; post village in Somerset County on the New York, Philadelphia and Norfolk Railroad.

Hopkins; creek, a small branch of Middle River in Baltimore County.

Horn; point in Anne Arundel County, projecting into Annapolis Roads.

Horn; point in Dorchester County, projecting into Choptank River.

Horner; cove, a small inlet of West Fork of Langford Bay in Kent County.

Horning; run, a small branch of Bird River in Baltimore County.

Horse; creek, a branch of Ape Hole Creek in Somerset County.

Horse; small marshy island at mouth of Manklin Creek in Worcester County.

Horse; small marshy island in Assawoman Bay in Worcester County.

Horsebridge; creek, a small branch of Nassawango Creek in Wicomico County.

Horse Landing; creek, a small tributary of Patuxent River in St. Mary County.

Horsepen; branch, a small tributary of Prince George County.

Horseshoe; bend, a small inlet of St. Mary River in St. Mary County.

Horseshoe; point in Anne Arundel County, projecting into Chepapeake Bay.

Horseshoe; point in St. Mary County, projecting into St. Mary River.

Houstans; branch, a small tributary of Nanticoke River in Caroline County.

Howard; county, formed out of the northwest corner of Anne Arundel County, is bounded on the north by Carroll County, east by Baltimore and Anne Arundel counties, and southwest by Prince George and Montgomery counties. The surface is undulating, being completely intersected with spring branches flowing into larger streams. The area is 240 square miles, of which more than three-fourths, or 110,546 acres, was under cultivation in 1900. The population for the same year was 16,715. The county seat is Ellicott City. The average magnetic declination in the county in 1900 was 5° 15′ west. The annual rainfall commonly ranges between 45 and 50 inches, and the mean annual temperature between 50° and 55°.

Howard; wharf on St. Clement Bay in St. Mary County.

Howardsville; post village in Baltimore County.

Howell; point in Kent County, projecting into Chesapeake Bay.

Howell; point in Talbot county, projecting into Choptank River.

Hoyes; run, a small branch of Youghiogheny River in Garrett County.

Hoyes; post village in Garrett County.

Huddle; point in Anne Arundel County, projecting into Magothy River.

Hudson; creek, a small tributary of Choptank River in Dorchester County.

Hudson; post village in Dorchester County.

Hughesville; post village in Charles County on the Washington, Potomac and Chesapeake Railroad.

Hughletts; neck, a strip of land lying between Cabin and Secretary creeks in Dorchester County.

Humphrey; creek, a small tributary of Patapsco River in Baltimore County.

Huntersville; post village in St. Mary County.

Hunting; creek, a tributary of Patuxent River in Calvert County.

Hunting; creek, a small tributary of Miles River in Talbot County.

Hunting; creek, a small tributary of Monocacy River in Frederick County.

Huntingfield; creek, a small stream tributary to Chesapeake Bay in Kent County.

Huntingfield; point in Kent County, projecting into Chesapeake Bay.

Hunting Hill; post village in Montgomery County.

Huntingtown; post village in Calvert County.

Hurlock; post village in Dorchester County.

Hurry; post village in St. Mary County.

Hurst; creek, a small tributary of Choptank River in Dorchester County.

Hutton; creek, a small tributary of Wicomico River.

Hutton; post village in Garrett County on the Baltimore and Ohio Railroad.

Hyattstown; town in Montgomery County. Population, 81.

Hyattsville; town in Prince George County on the Baltimore and Ohio and the Chesapeake Beach railroads. Population, 1,222.

Hydes; post village in Baltimore County.

Hynesboro; village in Prince George County.

Hynson; post village in Caroline County.

Igleharts; village in Anne Arundel County on the Annapolis, Washington and Baltimore Railroad.

Ijamsville; post village in Montgomery County on the Baltimore and Ohio Railroad.

Ilchester; post village in Howard County on the Baltimore and Ohio Railroad.

Indian; creek, a tributary of Patuxent River on boundary between St. Mary and Charles counties.

Indian; creek, a small branch of Anacostia River in Prince George County.

Indian; creek, a small tributary of Choptank River in Dorchester County.

Indian; landing on Severn River in Anne Arundel County.

Indian; point in Talbot County, projecting into Harris Creek.

Indian; run, a small branch of Blackrock Run in Baltimore County.

Indianhead; post village in Charles County.

Indian Rock; small island in Susquehanna River in Cecil County.

Indian Springs; village in Washington County.

Ingleside; post village in Queen Anne County.

Inverness; post village in Somerset County.

Irish; creek, a small branch of Broad Creek in Talbot County.

Ironhill; post village in Cecil County on the Philadelphia, Baltimore and Washington Railroad.

Iron Ore; mountain ridge in Allegany County, extending into Pennsylvania.

Ironshire; post village in Worcester County on the Philadelphia, Baltimore and Washington Railroad.

Ironsides; post village in Charles County.

Island; branch, a small tributary of Deer Creek in Harford County.

Island; creek, a small tributary of Choptank River in Talbot County.

Island; creek, a small tributary of Chester River in Queen Anne County.

Island; creek, a small tributary of Sassafras River in Kent County.

Island; creek, a small tributary of Potomac River on St. George Island in St. Mary County.

Island; creek, a small stream tributary of Fishing Bay in Dorchester County.

Island; creek, a small tributary of Patuxent River in Calvert County.

Island; point in Worcester County, projecting into Newport Bay.

Island Creek; post village in Calvert County.

Isle of Wight; small bay at the mouth of St. Martin River in Worcester County, separated from the ocean by a sand bar.

Isle of Wight; island formed of a bit of elevated dry land in the sea marshes of Worcester County.

Israel; creek, a small branch of Monocacy River in Frederick County.

Issue; post village in Charles County.

Ivery; post village in Howard County.

Jabez; branch, a small tributary of Severn River in Anne Arundel County.

Jack; bay, a small arm of Patuxent River in Calvert County.

Jack; creek, a small tributary of Nanticoke River in Dorchester County.

Jackson; creek, a small tributary of Deer Creek in Harford County.

Jackson; run, small tributary of Georges Creek in Allegany County.

Jackson; station in Cecil County on the Baltimore and Ohio Railroad.

Jackson Creek; landing on Chester River in Queen Anne County.

Jacksonville; post village in Baltimore County.

Jacobs; nose, a point in Cecil County, projecting into mouth of Elkton River.

Jacobs Store; village in Anne Arundel County.

Jacobsville; village in Anne Arundel County.

James; island at mouth of Choptank River in Dorchester County.

James; point on James Island in Dorchester County, projecting into Cheaspeake Bay.

James; run, a small tributary of Bush River in Harford County.

James; post village in Dorchester County.

Janes; large marshy island in Tangier Sound in Somerset County.

Jarboesville; post village in St. Mary County.

Jarrett; creek, a small tributary of Chester River in Kent County.

Jarrettsville; post village in Harford County.

Jason; village in Somerset County.

Jefferson; village in Frederick County.

Jenkins; creek, a small tributary of Choptank River in Dorchester County.

Jenkins; creek, a small tributary of Little Annemessex River in Somerset County.

Jenkins; hill, a spur of Meadow Mountain in Garrett County separating Poplar Lick and Bear Pen runs.

Jenkins; point in Worcester County, projecting into St. Martin River.

Jenkins; post village in Baltimore County.

Jennings; post village in Garrett County.

Jennings; run, a tributary of Wills Creek in Allegany County.

Jersey; small marshy island near mouth of Little Annemessex River in Somerset County.

Jersey; village in Wicomico County.

Jerusalem; post village in Harford County.

Jessup; post village in Howard County on the Baltimore and Ohio Railroad.

Jesterville; post village in Wicomico County.

Jewell; post village in Anne Arundel County.

Joes Ridge; creek, a small stream on Smith Island in Somerset County flowing into Chesapeake Bay.

Johns Hammock; marsh in Assawoman Bay in Worcester County.

Johnson; bay, an arm of Chincoteague Bay in Worcester County.

Johnson; creek, a small stream flowing into Ape Hole Creek in Somerset County.

Johnson; small pond in Wicomico County drained by Beaverdam Creek, a tributary of Wicomico River.

Jones; creek, a small tributary of Annemessex River in Somerset County.

Jones; creek, a small tributary of Manokin River in Somerset County.

Jones; point in Calvert County, projecting into Patuxent River.

Jones; small pond in Wicomico County drained by Beaverdam Creek, a tributary of Wicomico River.

Jones; post village in Worcester County.

Jones; wharf on Patuxent River in St. Mary County.

Jones; wharf on St. Mary River in St. Mary County.

Jones Falls; creek, rises in Lake Roland and flows through Baltimore City into Northwest Harbor of Patapsco River.

Joppa; post village in Harford County on the Baltimore and Ohio Railroad.

Journey Cake; neck, a strip of land between Island Creek and Chester River in Queen Anne County.

Judith; point in Charles County, projecting into Patuxent River.

Kaese Mill; village in Garret County.

Kalmia; village in Harford County.

Kane; point in Dorchester County, projecting into Honga River.

Kaywood; point in St. Mary County, projecting into Potomac River.

Kearney; post village in Garrett County.

Kedge; straits, a passage between Smith Island and South Marsh in Somerset County.

Keedysville; town in Washington County on the Baltimore and Ohio Railroad. Population, 426.

Keenan; ridge, a spur of Town Hill Mountain in Allegany County.

Keene; broads, a small pond at head of St. John Creek in Dorchester County.

Keene; ditch, a small branch of Honga River in Dorchester County.

Keener; village in Baltimore County.

Keeptryst; post village in Washington County.

Kelso; gap in Backbone Mountain in Garrett County.

Kelly; point in Worcester County, projecting into Chincoteague Bay.

Kelly; village in Wicomico County.

Kemptown; village in Frederick County.

Kendall; post village in Garrett County.

Kennedyville; post village in Kent County on the Philadelphia, Baltimore and Washington Railroad.

Kensington; post village in Montgomery County on the Baltimore and Ohio Railroad. Population, 477.

Kent; county, organized in 1650, is one of the Eastern Shore counties, and is bounded on the east by the State of Delaware. It is a peninsula lying between Sassafras River, north, Chesapeake Bay, west, and Chester River, south and southeast. The surface is level, though not low, and rolls sufficiently to be well drained by the many creeks flowing into its bordering rivers and the bay. The area is 281 square miles, of which about three-fourths, or 138,947 acres was under cultivation in 1900. The county seat is Chestertown, with a population of 3,008 in 1900. The average magnetic declination in the county in 1900 was 5° 40′ west. The annual rainfall commonly ranges between 45 and 50 inches, and the mean annual temperature between 50° and 55°.

Kent; island in Chesapeake Bay in Queen Anne County.

Kent; landing on Kent Island in Chester River in Queen Anne County.

Kent; point in Queen Anne County, projecting into Eastern Bay.

Kent Island; narrows, a passage separating Kent Island from the mainland in Queen Anne County.

Kent Island; village in Queen Anne County on Kent Island.

Kenwood; village in Baltimore County on the Philadelphia, Baltimore and Washington Railroad.

Kerrick; swamp, a small stream flowing into Zekiah Swamp in Charles County.

Keyser; point in Worcester County, projecting into Isle of Wight Bay.

Keyser; post village in Garrett County.

Kings; creek, a small tributary of Bush River in Harford County.

Kings; creek, a small branch of East Fork of Langford Bay in Kent County.

Kings; creek, a tributary of Manokin River in Somerset County.

Kings Creek; station in Somerset County on the New York, Philadelphia and Norfolk Railroad.

Kingsley; post village in Montgomery County.

Kingston; post village in Somerset County on the New York, Philadelphia and Norfolk Railroad.

Kings Valley; post village in Montgomery County.

Kingsville; post village in Baltimore County.

Kirby; landing on Chester River in Kent County.

Kirby; wharf on Choptank River in Talbot County.

Kirkham; post village in Talbot County on the Baltimore, Chesapeake and Atlantic Railway.

Kitty; point in St. Mary County, projecting into Potomac River.

Klej Grange; post village in Worcester County.

Knapp; narrows, a narrow passage between Chesapeake Bay and Harris Creek in Talbot County.

Knight Island; village in Cecil County.

Knoebel; post village in Baltimore County.

Knot; point in Worcester County, projecting into Newport Bay.

Knoxville; post village in Frederick County on the Baltimore and Ohio Railroad.

Koontz; run, a small tributary of Georges Creek in Garrett County.

Koontz; village in Allegany County on the George's Creek and Cumberland Railroad.

Kreigbaum; station in Allegany County on the Cumberland and Pennsylvania Railroad.

Krug; station in Garrett County on the Baltimore and Ohio Railroad.

Kump; post village in Carroll County.

Ladiesburg; post village in Frederick County.

Lakeland; post village in Prince George County on the Baltimore and Ohio Railroad.

Lake Ogleton; small inlet of Annapolis Roads in Anne Arundel County.

Lake Roland; small lake in Baltimore County drained by Jones Falls.

Lakeshore; post village in Anne Arundel County.

Lakesville; post village in Dorchester County.

Lambson; village in Kent County on the Philadelphia, Baltimore and Washington Railroad.

Lamotte; post village in Carroll County.

Lancaster; wharf on Wicomico River in Charles County.

Lander; post village in Frederick County.

Landonville; post village in Somerset County.

Landover; post village in Prince George County on Philadelphia, Baltimore and Washington Railroad.

Lane; creek, a small tributary of West River in Anne Arundel County.

Lanes; run, a small branch of Licking Creek in Washington County.

Langford; bay, a creek tributary to Chester River in Kent County.

Langford; post village in Kent County.

Lanham; post village in Prince George County.

Lansdown; post village in Baltimore County on the Baltimore and Ohio Railroad.

Lantz; post village in Frederick County.

Lapidum; post village in Harford County.

Laplata; county seat of Charles County on the Philadelphia, Baltimore and Washington Railroad.

Largo; post village in Prince George County.

Lauraville; village in Baltimore County.

Laurel; run, a small tributary of Buffalo Run in Garrett County.

Laurel; run, a small tributary of Little Elk Creek in Cecil County.

Laurel; run, a small tributary of North Branch of Potomac River in Garrett County.

Laurel; run, a small tributary of Youghiogheny River in Garrett County.

Laurel; run, rises in Garrett County and flows through Allegany County into Georges Creek.

Laurel; town in Prince George County on the Baltimore and Ohio Railroad. Population, 2,079.

Laurel Brook; station in Harford County on the Maryland and Pennsylvania Railroad.

Laurel Grove; post village in St. Mary County.

Lavender Hill; village in Baltimore County.

Laws; thoroughfare, a passageway separating Deal Island from the mainland in Somerset County.

Lawsonia; post village in Somerset County.

Lawyers; cove, a small inlet of Langford Bay in Kent County.

Layhill; post village in Montgomery County.

Laytonsville; town in Montgomery County. Population, 148.

Lazaretto; point in Baltimore County, projecting into Patapsco River.

Leadenham; creek, a small tributary of Broad Creek in Talbot County.

Leading; point in Anne Arundel County, projecting into Patapsco River. A lighthouse is erected thereon.

Le Compt; bay, a small inlet of Choptank River in Dorchester County.

Lee; creek, a small tributary of Choptank River in Dorchester County.

Leeds; creek, a small tributary of Miles River in Talbot County.

Leeds; post village in Cecil County.

Leeland; post village in Prince George County on the Philadelphia, Baltimore and Ohio Railroad.

Lego; point in Harford County, projecting into Bush River.

Le Gore; post village in Frederick County on the Northern Central Railway.

Leitch; wharf on Patuxent River in Calvert County.

Leitchs; post village in Anne Arundel County.

Lelland; village in Prince George County on the Philadelphia, Baltimore and Washington Railroad.

Leon; post village in Anne Arundel County.

Leonard; small pond in Wicomico County drained by Wicomico River.

Leonardtown; county seat of St. Mary County. Population, 463.

Leslie; post village in Cecil County on the Baltimore and Ohio Railroad.

Level; post village in Harford County.

Lewis; knob, a mountain in Garrett County. Height, 2,000 feet.

Lewis; landing on Nanticoke River in Dorchester County.

Lewisdale; post village in Montgomery County.

Lewistown; village in Frederick County.

Liberty Grove; post village in Cecil County on the Philadelphia, Baltimore and Washington Railroad.

Libertytown; small branch of Timmonstown Branch in Worcester County.

Libertytown; village in Frederick County.

Licking; creek, a tributary of Potomac River in Washington County.

Licking; run, a small branch of Deep Run on boundary between Howard and Anne Arundel counties.

Licksville; village in Frederick County.

Lighting Knot; cove in Smith Island in Somerset County.

Limekiln; post village in Frederick County.

Linchester; post village in Caroline County.

Linden; village in Montgomery County on the Baltimore and Ohio Railroad.

Linden; village in Prince George County on the Philadelphia, Baltimore and Washington Railroad.

Lineboro; post village in Carroll County.

Linganore; village in Frederick County.

Linkwood; post village in Dorchester County on the Philadelphia, Baltimore and Washington Railroad.

Linthicum; village in Anne Arundel County on the Baltimore and Annapolis Short Line Railroad.

Linwood; post village in Carroll County on the Western Maryland Railroad.

Lisbon; post village in Howard County.

Little; creek, a small tributary to Monie Bay in Somerset County.

Little; creek, a small tributary of Choptank River in Talbot County.

Little; small marshy island in Tangier Sound in Somerset County.

Little; mountain in Garrett County.

Little; pond in Worcester County near head of Swan Gut Creek.

Little Allegany; mountain, on border between Pennsylvania and Maryland in Allegany County.

Little Annemessex; river, a tributary to Tangier Sound in Somerset County.

Little Bennett; creek, a small tributary of Big Bennett Creek in Frederick County.

Little Blackwater; river, a tributary of Blackwater River in Dorchester County.

Little Bohemia; creek, a tributary of Bohemia River in Cecil County.

Little Buffalo; run, a small branch of Buffalo Run in Garrett County.

Little Burnt; branch, a small tributary of Wicomico River in Wicomico County.

Little Catoctin; creek, a small tributary of Potomac River in Frederick County.

Little Choptank; river, tributary to Chesapeake Bay in Dorchester County.

Little Cove; point in Calvert County, projecting into Chesapeake Bay.

Little Deer; creek, a small tributary of Deer Creek in Harford County.

Little Egging; beach on sand bar separating Sinepuxent Bay from the Atlantic Ocean in Worcester County.

Little Elk; creek, heads in Pennsylvania and flows through Cecil County into Elk River.

Little Falls; creek, a tributary of Gunpowder Falls in Baltimore County.

Little Gunpowder Falls; river, a tributary of Gunpowder River on boundary between Baltimore and Harford counties.

Little Hunting; creek, a branch of Hunting Creek in Frederick County.

Little Laurel; run, a small branch of South Branch of Castleman River.

Little Magothy; river, a tributary of Magothy River in Anne Arundel County.

Little Monie; creek, a tributary to Monie Bay in Somerset County.

Little Monocacy; river, a tributary of Monocacy River in Montgomery County.

Little Northeast; creek, a branch of Northeast River in Cecil County.

Little Orleans; post village in Allegany County.

Little Patuxent; river, tributary of Big Patuxent River in Howard and Anne Arundel counties.

Little Pipe; creek, a tributary of Big Pipe Creek on boundary between Frederick and Carroll counties.

Little Point; creek, a branch of Point Branch in Prince George County.

Little Round; bay, a small inlet of Big Round Bay in Anne Arundel County.

Little Run; creek, a small branch of Little Pipe Creek in Carroll County.

Little Savage; mountain, a ridge lying parallel to Big Savage Mountain in Garrett County, extending into Pennsylvania.

Little Savage; river, a tributary of Savage River in Garrett County.

Little Seneca; creek, a tributary of Great Seneca Creek in Montgomery County.

Little Shade; run, a tributary of Big Shade Run in Garrett County.

Little Tonoloway; creek, a tributary of Tonoloway Creek in Washington County.

Little Troy; small island at mouth of Sawney Cove in Somerset County.

Little Tuscarora; creek, a small tributary of Monocacy River in Frederick County.

Little Youghiogheny; river, a tributary of Youghiogheny River in Garrett County.

Lloyd; creek, a small tributary of Sassafras River in Kent County.

Lloyd; creek, a small tributary of Front Wye River in Talbot County.

Lloyds; point in Baltimore County, projecting into mouth of Humphrey Creek.

Lloyds; post village in Dorchester County.

Loarville; village in Allegany County.

Loch Raven; post village in Baltimore County on the Maryland and Pennsylvania Railroad.

Loch Lynn Heights; town in Garrett County.   Population, 215.

Lock 53; village in Washington County.

Lockearn; village in Baltimore County.

Locust; point in Cecil County, projecting into Chesapeake Bay.

Locust; point in Cecil County, projecting into Elk River.

Locust; point in Harford County, projecting into Chesapeake Bay.

Locust; point in Somerset County, projecting into Manokin River.

Locustgrove; post village in Kent County.

Loderick; creek, a small tributary of Bush River in Harford County.

Log; point in Baltimore County, projecting into Middle River.

Lombard; post village in Cecil County.

Lonaconing; town in Allegany County on the Cumberland and Pennsylvania and George's Creek and Cumberland railroads.   Population, 2,181.

Lone Cedar; point in Worcester County, projecting into Assawoman Bay.

Lonehouse; creek, a small tributary of South River in Anne Arundel County.

Long; cove, a small inlet of Langford Bay in Kent County.

Long; small island in Susquehanna River in Cecil County.

Long; small, almost entirely marshy island in Chesapeake Bay in Dorchester County.

Long; hollow in Tonoloway Ridge in Washington County.

Long; point in Anne Arundel County, projecting into Round Bay.

Long; point in Dorchester County, projecting into Nanticoke River.

Long; point in Dorchester County, projecting into Honga River.

Long; point in Queen Anne County, projecting into Chester River.

Long; point in St. Mary County, projecting into St. Clements Bay.

Long; point in St. Mary County, projecting into St. Mary River.

Long; point in St. Mary County, projecting into Patuxent River.

Long; point in Somerset County, projecting into Big Annemessex River.

Long; point in Somerset County, projecting into mouth of Wicomico River.

Long; point in Somerset County, projecting into Little Annemessex River.

Long; point in Talbot County, projecting into Miles River.

Long; post village in Allegany County.

Long; mountain ridge in Washington County lying between Tonoloway Ridge and Sideling Hill.

Long Corner; a village in Howard County.

Long Draught; creek, a tributary of Great Seneca Creek in Montgomery County.

Long Green; creek, a tributary of Gunpowder Falls in Baltimore County.

Long Green; post village in Baltimore County on the Maryland and Pennsylvania Railroad.

Longhaul; creek, a small tributary of Miles River in Talbot County.

Long Marsh; ditch, a small tributary of Tuckahoe Creek on boundary of Queen Anne and Caroline counties.

Longrell; creek, a small tributary of Nanticoke River in Dorchester County.

Longwoods; post village in Talbot County.

Look-in; point in St. Mary County, projecting into Chesapeake Bay.

Lookout; point in St. Mary County, projecting into mouth of Potomac River.

Lord; post village in Allegany County.

Lorddolph; village in Allegany County.

Loreley; post village in Baltimore County on the Baltimore and Ohio Railroad.

Loretto; village in Somerset County on the New York, Philadelphia and Norfolk Railroad.

Lost Sand; run, a small tributary of North Branch of Potomac River in Garrett County.

Lothian; post village in Anne Arundel County.

Lottsford; small branch of Western Branch in Prince George County.

Love; point in Queen Anne County, projecting into Chester River.

Love; run, a small tributary of Octararo Creek in Cecil County.

Lovell; point in Baltimore County, projecting into Patapsco River.

Lovely; cove, a small inlet of East Fork of Langford Bay in Kent County.

Lovers; point in St. Mary County, projecting into Breton Bay.

Loveville; post village in St. Mary County.

Lower Cedar; point in Charles County, projecting into Potomac River.

Lower Island; point in Baltimore County, projecting into Chesapeake Bay.

Lower Hunting; creek, a small tributary of Upper Hunting Creek in Dorchester County.

Lower Marlboro; post village in Calvert County.

Lower Spaniards; point in Queen Anne County, projecting into Chester River.

Lower Thorn; point in Charles County, projecting into Potomac River.

Lower Thoroughfare; passageway separating Little Island from Deal Island in Somerset County.

Lowndes; village in Allegany County.

Lows; landing on Eastern Bay in Talbot County.

Lows; point in Talbot County, projecting into Eastern Bay.

Loys; post village in Frederick County on the Western Maryland Railroad.

Luce; creek, a small tributary of Severn River in Anne Arundel County.

Luke; post village in Allegany County.

Lumber; small marshy island in Chincoteague Bay in Worcester County.

Lusbys; post village in Calvert County.

Lutherville; post village in Baltimore County on the Northern Central Railway.

Lydia; post village in Washington County.

Lynch; point in Baltimore County, projecting into Back River.

Lynch; post village in Kent County on the Philadelphia, Baltimore and Washington Railroad.

Lyons; creek, a small tributary of Patuxent River on boundary between Calvert and Anne Arundel counties.

Lyons Creek; wharf on Patuxent River in Calvert County.

McConchie; post village in Charles County.

McCoole; post village in Allegany County.

McDameltown; village in Talbot County.

McDaniel; post village in Talbot County on the Baltimore, Chesapeake and Atlantic Railway.

McDonogh; post village in Baltimore County on the Western Maryland Railroad.

McHenry; post village in Garrett County.

McIntosh; run, a small tributary to Breton Bay in St. Mary County.

McIntyre; village in Harford County.

McKendree; post village in Anne Arundel County.

McKendree; village in Prince George County.

Mackall; post village in Calvert County.

Macton; post village in Harford County.

Macum; small tributary of Chester River in Queen Anne County.

Maddox; island, a bit of elevated dry land in sea marshes of Somerset County.

Maddox; post village in St. Mary County.

Madison; bay, a small inlet of Little Choptank River in Dorchester County.

Madison; post village in Dorchester County.

Madonna; village in Harford County.

Magnolia; post village in Harford County on the Philadelphia, Baltimore and Washington Railroad.

Magothy; river, an estuary entering Chesapeake Bay in Anne Arundel County.

Magruder; small branch of Great Seneca Creek in Montgomery County.

Magruder; (Tuxedo P. O.) village in Prince George County on Philadelphia, Baltimore and Washington Railroad.

Main; creek, a small tributary of Patapsco River in Anne Arundel County.

Malcolm; post village in Charles County.

Mallows; creek, a small tributary of Potomac River in Charles County.

Manahowic; creek, a small tributary of Wicomico River in St. Mary County.

Manchester; village in Carroll County.   Population, 609.

Manklin; creek, a small tributary to Isle of Wight Bay in Worcester County.

Manokin; post village in Somerset County.

Manokin; river, a tributary to Tangier Sound in Somerset County.

Manor; post village in Baltimore County.

Mantua; village in Baltimore County.

Maple; run, a small branch of Town Creek in Allegany County.

Maplegrove; post village in Carroll County on the Western Maryland Railroad.

Mapleville; post village in Washington County.

Marble Hill; village in Baltimore County.

Mardela Springs; post village in Wicomico County on the Baltimore, Chesapeake and Atlantic Railway.

Margots; small island in St. Martin River in Worcester County.

Marion; post village in Somerset County on the New York, Philadelphia and Norfolk Railroad.

Marlboro; station in Prince George County on the Philadelphia, Baltimore and Washington Railroad.

Marley; creek, a tributary of Curtis Creek in Anne Arundel County.

Marley; post village in Anne Arundel County on the Baltimore and Annapolis Short Line Railroad.

Marriott Hill; village in Anne Arundel County.

Marriottsville; post village in Howard County on the Baltimore and Ohio Railroad.

Marsh; creek, a small branch of Back Creek in Baltimore County

Marsh; creek, a small tributary of Choptank River in Caroline County.

Marsh; hill in Garrett County.   Height, 3,073 feet.

Marsh; point in Kent County, projecting into Island Creek.

Marsh; point in St. Mary County, projecting into Patuxent River.

Marsh; run, a branch of Deep Creek in Garrett County.

Marshall; creek, a small tributary to Newport Bay in Worcester County.

Marshall Hall; post village in Charles County.

Marshy; creek, a small tributary to Prospect Bay in Queen Anne County.

Marter; cove, a small inlet of Wye River in Queen Anne County.

Martin; bay, an arm of Chincoteague Bay in Worcester County.

Martin; mountain ridge in Allegany County extending into Pennsylvania.

Martin; point in Worcester County, projecting into Chincoteague Bay.

Martin; point in St. Mary County, projecting into St. Mary River.

Martinsburg; post village in Montgomery County.

Marumsco; creek, a tributary of Pocomoke River in Somerset County.

Marumsco; post village in Somerset County.

Marydell; post village in Caroline County on the Philadelphia, Baltimore and Washington Railroad.

Maryland; point in Charles County, projecting into Potomac River.

Maryland Line; post village in Baltimore County.

Masons; island in Potomac River in Montgomery County.

Mason Springs; post village in Charles County.

Massey; post village in Kent County on the Philadelphia, Baltimore and Washington Railroad.

Mataponi; creek, a small tributary of Patuxent River in Prince George County.

Mattapex; post village in Queen Anne County.

Mattaponi; landing on Pocomoke River in Worcester County.

Mattawoman; creek, a tributary of Potomac River in Prince George and Charles counties.

Mattawoman; post village in Charles County.

Matthew; run, a small tributary of Georges Creek in Allegany County.

Matthews; post village in Talbot County.

Maugansville; post village in Washington County on the Cumberland Valley Railroad.

Mayfield; post village in Howard County.

Maynard; post village in Anne Arundel County.

Maynardier; ridge, a spur of Meadow Mountain separating Little and Big Laurel runs in Garrett County.

Mayo; point in Anne Arundel County, projecting into South River.

Mayo; post village in Anne Arundel County.

Meadow; small island in Susquehanna River in Harford County.

Meadow; mountain ridge in Garrett County. Height, 3,031 feet.

Meadow; run, a small tributary of Castleman River heading in Garrett County and flowing into Pennsylvania.

Meadow Mountain; run, a tributary of Deep Creek in Garrett County.

Meadows; post village in Prince George County.

Mechanicsville; post village in St. Mary County on the Washington, Potomac and Chesapeake Railroad.

Mechanic Valley; village in Cecil County.

Medford; post village in Carroll County on the Western Maryland Railroad.

Meekin; neck, a strip of land lying between Honga River and Chesapeake Bay in Dorchester County.

Melitota; post village in Kent County.

Melson; village in Wicomico County.

Melvale; village in Baltimore County on the Northern Central Railway.

Merrell; post village in Garrett County.

Michaelsville; post village in Harford County.

Middle; branch, a tributary of Patapsco River within limits of Baltimore City.

Middle; small branch of Shingle Landing Prong in Worcester County.

Middle; creek, a small stream on Deal Island in Somerset County tributary to Tangier Sound.

Middle; neck, a strip of land lying between Great and Little Bohemia creeks in Cecil County.

Middle; ridge, a spur of Meadow Mountain in Garrett County separating Monroe and Big runs.

Middle; river, a tributary to Chesapeake Bay in Baltimore County.

Middlebrook; post village in Montgomery County.

Middleburg; post village in Carroll County on the Western Maryland Railroad.

Middle Fork; creek, a tributary of Savage River in Garrett County.

Middle Patuxent; river in Howard County flowing into Little Patuxent River.

Middle Quarter; cove, a tributary of Chester River in Queen Anne County.

Middleriver; post village in Baltimore County on the Philadelphia, Baltimore and Washington Railroad.

Middletown; town in Frederick County.   Population, 665.

Midland; post village in Allegany County on the Cumberland and Pennsylvania Railroad.

Midlothian; post village in Allegany County on the Cumberland and Pennsylvania Railroad.

Milburn; landing on Pocomoke River in Worcester County.

Miles; branch, a tributary of Nanticoke River in Dorchester County.

Miles; river, a tributary to Eastern Bay in Talbot County.

Milestown; post village in St. Mary County.

Miley; creek, a small tributary to St. Clement Bay in St. Mary County.

Mill; brook, a tributary of Deer Creek in Harford County.

Mill; creek, a small branch of Furnace Creek in Cecil County.

Mill; creek, a small branch of Island Creek in Kent County.

Mill; creek, a small tributary of North Branch of Potomac River in Allegany County.

Mill; creek, a small branch of Rock Creek in Montgomery County.

Mill; creek, a small tributary of Whitehall River in Anne Arundel County.

Mill; creek, a small tributary of Patuxent River in Calvert County.

Mill; creek, a small tributary of Patuxent River in St. Mary County.

Mill; creek, a small tributary of Wicomico River in St. Mary County.

Mill; point in Dorchester County, projecting into Trappe Bay.

Mill; point in St. Mary County, projecting into Wicomico River.

Mill; run, a small tributary of Youghiogheny River.

Mill; run, a tributary of Georges Creek in Garrett and Allegany counties.

Miller; island in Chesapeake Bay in Baltimore County.

Miller; run, a small branch of Poplar Lick Run in Garrett County.

Miller; run, a small tributary of Youghiogheny River in Garrett County.

Miller; village in Allegany County.

Millers; post village in Carroll County on the Western Maryland Railroad.

Millersville; post village in Anne Arundel County on the Annapolis, Washington and Baltimore Railroad.

Millersville; village in Baltimore County on the Baltimore and Ohio Railroad.

Mill Green; village in Harford County.

Millington; town in Kent County on the Philadelphia, Baltimore and Washington Railroad.   Population, 406.

Mills; branch, a small tributary of Chester River in Kent County.

Mills; small island in Susquehanna River in Cecil County.

Mills; small, almost entirely marshy island in Chincoteague Bay in Worcester County.

Millstone; village in St. Mary County.

Millstone; village in Washington County.

Milltown; landing on Patuxent River in Prince George County.

Millville; village in Worcester County.

Milton; village in Dorchester County.

Milton; point in Kent County, projecting into Chester River.

Mine; creek, a small tributary of Manokin River in Somerset County.

Mine Bank; run, a small tributary of Gunpowder Falls in Baltimore County.

Mineral Spring; village in Garrett County.

Minksville; village in Wicomico County.

Mitchell; bluff, a point in Kent County, projecting into Chesapeake Bay.

Mitchellville; post village in Prince George County.

Moccasin; pond, a small inlet of Isle of Wight Bay in Worcester County.

Mockingbird; pond in Wicomico County drained by Barren Creek.

Mondel; post village in Washington County on the Norfolk and Western Railway.

Monie; bay, an arm of Chesapeake Bay in Somerset County.

Monie; neck, a strip of land lying between Big and Little Monie creeks and Monie Bay.

Monie; post village in Somerset County.

Monkey Lodge; hill in Garrett County. Height, 2,600 feet.

Monkton; post village in Baltimore County on the Northern Central Railway.

Monocacy; post village in Montgomery County.

Monocacy; river, a tributary of Potomac River in Frederick County.

Monroe; run, a small tributary of Big Run in Garrett County.

Monrovia; post village in Frederick County on the Baltimore and Ohio Railroad.

Montebello; small lake within the chartered limits of Baltimore City.

Montgomery; county, bounded on the southwest by Virginia, on the northwest by Frederick County, on the northeast by Patuxent River, and southeast by Prince George County and the District of Columbia. The surface is mostly hilly, and gives rise to many branches, most of which have considerable fall in a very short distance. The area is 400 square miles, of which nearly two-thirds, or 212,840 acres, was under cultivation in 1900. The county seat is Rockville, with a population of 1,110 in 1900. The average magnetic declination in the county in 1900 was 4° 45′ west. The annual rainfall commonly ranges between 45 and 50 inches, and the mean annual temperature between 50° and 55°.

Montrose; post village in Montgomery County.

Moon; mountain ridge in Garrett County.

Moons; bay, a small inlet of Big Annemessex River in Somerset County.

Moore; knob, a hill in Washington County. Height, 900 feet.

Moore; run, a small tributary of Georges Creek in Allegany County.

Moors; run, a small tributary of Back River in Baltimore County.

Morantown; village in Allegany County.

Morgan; creek, a small tributary of Chester River in Kent County.

Morgan; post village in Carroll County on the Baltimore and Ohio Railroad.

Morgan; run, a small tributary of North Branch of Patapsco River in Carroll County.

Morganza; post village in St. Mary County.

Morgnec; post village in Kent County.

Morris; pond in Wicomico County drained by Morris Prong, which flows into Tonytank Creek.

Morris; prong, a small tributary of Tonytank Creek in Wicomico County.

Moscow Mill; post village in Allegany County.

Mosquito; creek, a small tributary of Chesapeake Bay in Harford County.

Motters; post village in Frederick County on the Emmitsburg Railroad.

Mountain; small branch of Winters Run in Harford County.

Mountain; point in Anne Arundel County, projecting into mouth of Magothy River.
Mountain; post village in Harford County.
Mountain Hill; village in Harford County.
Mountain Lake Park; town in Garrett County on the Baltimore and Ohio Railroad. Population, 215.
Mountain View; village in Howard County.
Mount Airy; village in Carroll County on the Baltimore and Ohio Railroad. Population, 332.
Mount Carmel; post village in Baltimore County.
Mount Ephraim; village in Montgomery County.
Mount Harmony; post village in Calvert County on the Chesapeake Beach Railway.
Mount Holly; village in Dorchester County.
Mount Hope; village in Baltimore County on the Western Maryland Railroad.
Mount Misery; village in Anne Arundel County.
Mount Pleasant; village in Frederick County.
Mount Savage; post village in Allegany County on the Cumberland and Pennsylvania Railroad.
Mount Savage Junction; station in Allegany County on the Baltimore and Ohio and the Cumberland and Pennsylvania railroads.
Mount Vernon; post village in Somerset County.
Mountview; post village in Howard County.
Mount Vista; post village in Baltimore County.
Mount Washington; village in Baltimore County.
Mount Wilson; post village in Baltimore County on the Western Maryland Railroad.
Mount Zion; village in Cecil County.
Mud; creek, a small tributary of Patuxent River in St. Mary County.
Mud; creek, a small tributary of Tred Avon River in Talbot County.
Mud; creek, a small tributary of Turville Creek in Worcester County.
Muddy; branch, a tributary of Potomac River in Montgomery County.
Muddy; creek, a small tributary of Big Annemessex River in Somerset County.
Muddy; creek, a small tributary of Chester River in Queen Anne County.
Muddy; creek, a small tributary of Choptank River in Talbot County.
Muddy; creek, a small tributary of Rhode River in Anne Arundel County.
Muddy; creek, a small tributary of Youghiogheny River in Garrett County.
Muddy; run, a small tributary of Herrington Creek in Garrett County.
Mudlick; hollow in Town Hill in Allegany County.
Muirkirk; post village in Prince George County on the Baltimore and Ohio Railroad.
Mulberry; point in Dorchester County, projecting into Nanticoke River.
Mulberry; point in Harford County, projecting into Chesapeake Bay.
Mullinix; post village in Montgomery County.
Murley; branch, a small tributary of Town Creek in Allegany County.
Murumsco; creek, a small tributary of Pocomoke River in Somerset County.
Muskrattown; village in Worcester County.
Mutton; small islands in Susquehanna River in Harford County.
Mutual; post village in Calvert County.
Myersville; post village in Frederick County.
My Lady; small branch of Carroll Branch in Baltimore County.
Myrtle; point in Somerset County, projecting into Big Annemessex River.
Nabs; creek, a small branch of Stony Creek in Anne Arundel County.
Nailors; small pond at junction of Little Burnt Branch and Wicomico River in Wicomico County.
Nan; cove, a small inlet of Patuxent River in Calvert County.
Nanjemoy; creek, a small tributary of Potomac River in Charles County.

Nanjemoy; post village in Charles County.

Nanticoke; point in Wicomico County, projecting into Wicomico River.

Nanticoke; post village in Wicomico County.

Nanticoke; river, heads in southern Delaware in several branches and flows southwest through Maryland into Tangier Sound, an arm of Chesapeake Bay.

Narrow; point in Queen Anne County, projecting into Prospect Bay.

Nassawango; large creek flowing through Wicomico and Worcester counties into Pocomoke River.

Nat; creek, a small branch of Mill Creek in St. Mary County.

Neal; sound, a narrow passage between the mainland and a small island in Charles County.

Neavitt; post village in Talbot County.

Nebo; mountain, a summit west of Savage River in Garrett County.

Necker; post village in Baltimore County.

Neelsville; village in Montgomery County.

Neff; run, a small tributary of Georges Creek in Allegany County.

Negro; mountain in Garrett County. Height, 2,800 feet.

Nelson; branch, a small tributary of Little Gunpowder Falls in Baltimore County.

Nelson; point in Talbot County, projecting into Choptank River.

Neri; post village in Allegany County.

Newark; post village in Worcester County.

Newburg; post village in Charles County.

Newcomb; creek, a small tributary of Miles River in Talbot County.

Newcomb; post village in Talbot County.

New Germany; post village in Garrett County.

New Glatz; post village in Prince George County.

Newhope; pond, a small inlet of Pocomoke River in Wicomico County.

Newhope; post village in Wicomico County.

New London; village in Frederick County.

New Market; town in Frederick County. Population, 360.

New Midway; post village in Frederick County on the Northern Central Railway.

Newport; bay, a small arm of Chincoteague Bay in Worcester County.

Newport; creek, a small branch of Trappe Creek in Worcester County.

Newport; neck, a strip of land lying between Spencer Cove and Trappe Creek in Worcester County.

Newport; post village in Charles County.

New Step; small branch of Horsepen Branch in Prince George County.

Newton; post village in Caroline County.

Newtown; neck, a narrow strip of land between Breton and St. Clement bays in St. Mary County.

Newtown; village in Kent County.

New Valley; village in Cecil County.

New Windsor; town in Carroll County on the Western Maryland Railroad. Population, 430.

Nichols; small mountain ridge in Allegany County.

Nicholson; village in Kent County on the Philadelphia, Baltimore and Washington Railroad.

Niles Mill; village in Garrett County.

Ninepin Bridge; creek, a tributary of Pocomoke River in Worcester County.

Norbeck; post village in Montgomery County.

Norman; cove, a small inlet at mouth of Honga River in Dorchester County.

Norman; creek, a small tributary of Middle River in Baltimore County.

Norman; post village in Queen Anne County.

Norrisville; post village in Harford County.

North; small branch of Laurel Run in Garrett County.

North; branch, a tributary of Castleman River in Garrett County.

North; branch, a small tributary of Rock Creek in Montgomery County.

North; fork, a branch of Crabtree Creek in Garrett County.

North; fork, a small branch of Bens Branch in Frederick County.

North; fork, a small branch of Linganore Creek in Frederick County.

North; fork, a small branch of Sand Branch in Garrett County.

North; point in Talbot County, projecting into Eastern Bay.

North; run, a small tributary of South River in Anne Arundel County.

North Branch; village in Allegany County on the Baltimore and Ohio Railroad.

Northbranch; post village in Baltimore County.

North Branch of Patapsco; river on boundary of Carroll and Baltimore counties, tributary to Patapsco River.

North Branch of Potomac; river, the head branch of Potomac River, forming part of boundary between Maryland and West Virginia.

Northeast; branch, a small tributary to Harris Bay in Talbot County.

Northeast; small branch of Western Branch in Prince George County.

Northeast; cove, a small inlet of Holland Straits in Dorchester County.

Northeast; creek, a small tributary of Back River in Baltimore County.

Northeast; creek, a small tributary of Northeast River in Cecil County.

Northeast; small marshy island in Holland Straits in Dorchester County.

Northeast; river, a tributary to Chesapeake Bay in Cecil County.

Northeast; town in Cecil County. Population, 969.

North Glade; run, a small branch of Deep Creek in Garrett County.

Northkey; post village in Prince George County.

North Point; creek, a small tributary to Old Road Bay in Baltimore County.

Northpoint; post village in Baltimore County on the Philadelphia, Baltimore and Washington Railroad.

Northwest; branch, a small tributary of Anacostia River in Prince George County.

Northwest; branch, a small tributary to Harris Bay in Talbot County.

Northwest; harbor, an inlet of Patapsco River within limits of Baltimore City.

Norwood; post village in Montgomery County.

Notch Cliff; village in Baltimore County on the Maryland and Pennsylvania Railroad.

Notre Dame; station in Baltimore County on the Maryland and Pennsylvania Railroad.

Nottingham; post village in Prince George County.

Nutwell; post village in Anne Arundel County.

Nydegger; run, a small tributary of North Branch of Potomac River in Garrett County.

Oak; creek, a small branch of Miles Creek in Talbot County.

Oak; small marshy island in Assawoman Bay in Worcester County.

Oak Crest; village in Prince George County on Baltimore and Ohio Railroad.

Oakdale; post village in Montgomery County.

Oak Grove; village in Prince George County.

Oakington; village in Harford County on the Philadelphia, Baltimore and Washington Railroad.

Oakland; county seat of Garrett County on the Baltimore and Ohio Railroad. Poplation, 1,170.

Oakland; village in Baltimore County.

Oakland Mills; post village in Howard County.

Oakley; post village in St. Mary County.

Oaks; village in St. Mary County.

Oakville; post village in St. Mary County.

Oakwood; post village in Cecil County.

Observatory; hill, a summit in Little Mountain in Garrett County. Elevation, 2,767 feet.

Ocean; post village in Allegany County on the Cumberland and Pennsylvania Railroad.

Ocean City; town in Worcester County on the Baltimore, Chesapeake and Atlantic Railway. Population, 365.

Octoraro; creek, a tributary of Susquehanna River rising in Pennsylvania and flowing through Cecil County.

Octoraro; village in Cecil County on the Philadelphia, Baltimore and Washington Railroad.

Odenton; post village in Anne Arundel County on the Annapolis, Washington and Baltimore and the Philadelphia, Baltimore and Washington railroads.

Oella; post village in Baltimore County on the Baltimore and Ohio Railroad.

Old Field; point in Kent County, projecting into Sassafras River.

Oldfield; point in Cecil County, projecting into Elk River.

Old Germantown; village in Montgomery County.

Old House; cove, a small inlet of Little Annemessex River in Somerset County.

Old Mill; branch, a small tributary of Pocomoke River in Worcester County.

Old Road; bay, a small inlet of Patapsco River in Baltimore County.

Oldtown; post village in Allegany County.

Old Womans; gut, a small inlet of Chesapeake Bay in Harford County.

Oliver; point in Baltimore County, projecting into Gunpowder River.

Olivet; post village in Calvert County.

Olney; post village in Montgomery County.

Omar; post village in Anne Arundel County.

Ona; small branch of Big Pipe Creek in Carroll County.

Ordinary; point in Cecil County, projecting into Sassafras River.

Oregon; village in Baltimore County.

Oriole; post village in Somerset County.

Orme; post village in Prince George County.

Osborne; village in Harford County on the Philadelphia, Baltimore and Washington and the Baltimore and Ohio railroads.

Otter; creek, a small stream on Smith Island in Somerset County tributary to Chesapeake Bay.

Otter; small marshy island in Tangier Sound in Somerset County.

Otter; point in St. Mary County, projecting into Chesapeake Bay.

Otter Point; creek, a small tributary of Bush River in Harford County.

Outward Tump; small marshy island in Chincoteague Bay in Worcester County.

Overshot; run, a small tributary of Big Gunpowder Falls in Baltimore County.

Overton; post village in Kent County.

Owens; creek, a small tributary of Nanticoke River in Dorchester County.

Owing Mills; post village in Baltimore County on the Western Maryland Railroad.

Owings; post village in Talbot County on the Chesapeake Beach Railway.

Owl; branch, a small tributary of Little Falls Creek in Baltimore County.

Oxenhill; post village in Prince George County.

Oxford; town in Talbot County on the Philadelphia, Baltimore and Washington Railroad. Population, 1,243.

Oxon; village in Prince George County.

Oyster; cove, a small inlet of Chester River.

Oyster; creek, a small tributary to Kedge Strait in Somerset County.

Oyster; small pond in marshes of Worcester County.

Oyster Shell; creek, a small tributary of Choptank River in Dorchester County.

Pagan; point in St. Mary County, projecting into St. Mary River.

Palmers; post village in St. Mary County on the Queen Anne's Railroad.

Palmetto; village in Somerset County.

Pamosa; post village in Allegany County.

Panther; branch, a small tributary of Gunpowder Falls in Baltimore County.

Paradise; village in Allegany County on the Philadelphia, Baltimore and Washington Railroad.

Paramount; post village in Washington County.

Parish; creek, a small tributary of West River in Anne Arundel County.

Parker; bay, an arm of Chincoteague Bay in Worcester County.

Parker; branch, a small tributary of Little Gunpowder Falls in Baltimore County.

Parker; creek, a small tributary to Chesapeake Bay in Calvert County.

Parker; small island in Herring Bay in Anne Arundel County.

Parker; neck, a narrow strip of land lying between Charles Creek and Honga River in Dorchester County.

Parkhall; post village in St. Mary County.

Park Mills; village in Frederick County.

Parkton; post village in Baltimore County on the Northern Central Railway.

Parole; post village in Anne Arundel County.

Parran; post village in Calvert County.

Parson; creek, a small tributary of Patuxent River in St. Mary County.

Parson; small island in Eastern Bay in Queen Anne County.

Parsonsburg; post village in Wicomico County on the Baltimore, Chesapeake and Atlantic Railway.

Patapsco; river, a broad estuary whose head forms the harbor of Baltimore City and connects that city with Chesapeake Bay.

Patapsco; station in Anne Arundel County on the Philadelphia, Baltimore and Washington Railroad.

Patapsco; station in Baltimore County on the Baltimore and Ohio Railroad.

Patapsco; post village in Carroll County on the Western Maryland Railroad.

Patapsco River; neck, a strip of land lying between Back and Patapsco rivers in Baltimore County.

Patience; point in Calvert County, projecting into Patuxent River.

Patterson; creek, a small tributary of North Branch of Potomac River in Allegany County.

Patterson Creek; mountain ridge separating Patterson Creek and Dan Run in Allegany County.

Pattys; branch, a small tributary of Pocomoke River in Worcester County.

Patuxent; river, a tributary of Chesapeake Bay.

Patuxent; village in Anne Arundel County on the Philadelphia, Baltimore and Washington Railroad.

Patuxent; village in Charles County.

Passerdyke; creek, a tributary of Wicomico Creek on boundary between Wicomico and Somerset counties.

Pawn; run, a small tributary of Deep Creek in Garrett County.

Pawpaw; cove, a small inlet of Chesapeake Bay in Talbot County.

Pawpaw; creek, a small tributary of Chincoteague Bay in Worcester County.

Pawpaw; point in St. Mary County, projecting into Breton Bay.

Pea; ridge, a spur of Big Savage Mountain separating Bluelick and Muddick runs in Garrett County.

Peach; point in Worcester County, projecting into St. Martin River.

Peachblossom; creek, a small tributary of Tred Avon River in Talbot County.

Peapatch; ridge, a spur of Meadow Mountain separating Big and Bear Pen runs in Garrett County.

Pearce; creek, a small tributary of Elk River in Cecil County.

Pearce; neck, a strip of land between Cabin John and Pearce creeks in Cecil County.

Pearl; branch, a small tributary of Chester River in Queen Anne County.

Pearre; post village in Washington County.

Pearson; post village in St. Mary County.

Pecks; creek, a small tributary to Assawoman Bay in Worcester County.

Pecktonville; village in Washington County.

Peddler; run, a small tributary of Susquehanna River in Harford County.

Pekin; post village in Allegany County.

Peninsula Junction; post village in Somerset County.

Pen Knife; point in Dorchester County, projecting into Nanticoke River.

Perch; creek, a small tributary of Elk River in Cecil County.

Perkins; creek, a small tributary of Shingle Landing Prong in Worcester County.

Perryhall; post village in Baltimore County.

Perryman; post village in Harford County on the Philadelphia, Baltimore and Washington Railroad.

Perryville; town in Cecil County on the Pennsylvania and the Philadelphia, Baltimore and Washington railroads. Population, 770.

Persimmon; creek, a small tributary of Patuxent River in St. Mary County.

Persimmon; small island in Susquehanna River in Cecil County.

Persimmon; point in Anne Arundel County, projecting into Magothy River.

Persimmon; point in Somerset County, projecting into Big Annemessex River.

Peters; creek, a small tributary of Quantico Creek in Wicomico County.

Peters; run, a small branch of Town Creek in Allegany County.

Petersville; village in Frederick County.

Philip; creek, a small branch of East Fork of Langford Bay in Kent County.

Phillips; creek, a small tributary of Choptank River in Dorchester County.

Philopolis; post village in Baltimore County.

Phoenix; post village in Baltimore County on the Northern Central Railway.

Phoenix; village in Allegany County.

Piccowaxton; creek, a small tributary of Potomac River in Charles County.

Pickering; creek, a small tributary of Front Wye River in Talbot County.

Pigeon; creek, a small tributary to Monie Bay in Somerset County.

Pigskin; small mountain ridge in Washington County extending into Pennsylvania.

Pikes; creek, a small tributary of Chincoteague Bay in Worcester County.

Pikesville; village in Baltimore County.

Pilot; village in Cecil County.

Pindell; post village in Anne Arundel County on the Chesapeake Beach Railway.

Pine; hill, a summit in Garrett County. Elevation, 2,600 feet.

Pine; small mountain ridge in Allegany County.

Pine Hill; village in Baltimore County.

Pine Orchard; village in Howard County.

Pine Swamp; run, a small tributary of Savage River in Garrett County.

Piney; branch, a small tributary of Mattawoman Creek in Charles County.

Piney; branch, a small tributary of Patapsco River in Carroll County.

Piney; creek, a small tributary of Chester River in Queen Anne County.

Piney; creek, a small tributary of Gunpowder Falls in Baltimore County.

Piney; creek, a small tributary of Monocacy River in Carroll County.

Piney; creek, a small tributary to Pine Creek Cove in Cecil County.

Piney; small marshy island at mouth of Manokin River in Somerset County.

Piney; small marshy island in Assawoman Bay in Worcester County.

Piney; small island in St. Martin River in Worcester County.

Piney; neck, a strip of land lying between Wye River and Eastern Bay in Queen Anne County.

Piney; mountain, a part of the Allegany Front in Allegany County. Elevation, 2,407 feet.

Piney; point in Baltimore County, projecting into Middle River.

Piney; point in Harford County, projecting into Gunpowder River.

Piney; point in Kent County, projecting into Chester River.

Piney; point in Queen Anne County, projecting into Prospect Bay.

Piney; point in St. Mary County, projecting into Potomac River. A light-house is erected thereon.

Piney; ridge, a spur of Green Mountain in Allegany County.

Piney; run, a small branch of Licking Run in Anne Arundel County.

Piney; run, a small branch of Muddy Creek in Garrett County.

Piney; run, a small branch of Western Run in Baltimore County.

Piney; run, a small tributary of Patapsco River in Carroll County.

Piney Creek; cove, a small inlet of Elk River in Cecil County.

Pineygrove; post village in Allegany County.

Piney Island; cove, a small inlet of Tangier Sound in Dorchester County.

Pineypoint; post village in St. Mary County.

Piney Ridge; run, a small tributary of Fifteenmile Run in Allegany County.

Pinto; post village in Allegany County.

Piscataway; creek, a tributary of Potomac River in Prince George County.

Piscataway; post village in Prince George County. Population, 95.

Pisgah; post village in Charles County.

Pittsville; post village in Wicomico County on the Baltimore, Chesapeake and Atlantic Railway.

Plaindealing; creek, a small tributary of Tred Avon River in Talbot County.

Plane No. Four; post village in Frederick County on the Baltimore and Ohio Railroad.

Pleasanthill; post village in Cecil County.

Pleasantina; village in Anne Arundel County.

Pleasant Valley; run, a small tributary of North Branch of Castleman River in Garrett County.

Pleasantville; post village in Harford County.

Plowders; wharf on Wicomico River in St. Mary County.

Plum; branch, a small tributary of Nanticoke River in Dorchester County.

Plum; creek, a small tributary of Severn River in Anne Arundel County.

Plum; point in Calvert County, projecting into Chesapeake Bay.

Plum; point in Cecil County, projecting into Elk River.

Plum; point in Kent County, projecting into Chesapeake Bay.

Plumpoint; post village in Calvert County.

Plumtree; branch, a small tributary of Deer Creek in Harford County.

Plumtree; run, a small branch of Winters Run in Harford County.

Pocomoke; river on the peninsula heading in southern Delaware and flowing southwest into Chesapeake Bay.

Pocomoke City; town in Worcester County on the New York, Philadelphia, and Norfolk Railroad. Population, 2,124.

Point; branch, a small tributary of Anacostia River heading in Montgomery County and flowing through Prince George County.

Point; ridge, a spur of Jenkins Hill in Garrett County.

Point Lookout; creek, a small tributary of Potomac River in St. Mary County.

Point No Point; point in Dorchester County, projecting into Nanticoke River.

Point No Point; point in St. Mary County, projecting into Chesapeake Bay.

Point of Rocks; post village in Frederick County on the Baltimore and Ohio Railroad.

Polish; small mountain ridge in Allegany County.

Pomfret; post village in Charles County.

Pomona; post village in Kent County.

Pomonkey; creek, a small tributary of Potomac River in Charles County.

Pomonkey; post village in Charles County.

Pond; creek, a small tributary of Elk River in Cecil County.

Pond; neck, a strip of land lying between Pond and Pearce creeks in Cecil County.

Pond; point in St. Mary County, projecting into St. Mary River.

Pons; point in Dorchester County, projecting into Chesapeake Bay.

Pool; small, almost entirely marshy island in Chesapeake Bay in Kent County.

Poole; post village in Harford County.

Poolesville; town in Montgomery County.   Population, 236.

Pope; creek, a small tributary of Potomac River in Charles County.

Pope; small marshy island in Chincoteague Bay in Worcester County.

Pope Creek; post village in Charles County on the Philadelphia, Baltimore and Washington Railroad.

Poplar; harbor, a small inlet of Chesapeake Bay in Talbot County.

Poplar; island, a bit of elevated dry land in sea marshes of Dorchester County.

Poplar; small island in Chesapeake Bay in Talbot County.

Poplar; point in Worcester County, projecting into St. Martin River.

Poplar; village in Baltimore County on the Baltimore and Ohio Railroad.

Poplar Hill; creek, a small tributary of Potomac River in St. Mary County.

Poplar Lick; run, a small tributary of Savage River in Garrett County.

Poplars; post village in Calvert County.

Poplar Springs; post village in Howard County.

Porpoise; creek, a small tributary of Choptank River in Talbot County.

Porpoise; pond, a small inlet of Assawoman Bay in Worcester County.

Porter; sand bar in Back River in Baltimore County.

Porter; creek, a small tributary of Miles River in Talbot County.

Porter; village in Allegany County.

Port Deposit; town in Cecil County on the Philadelphia, Baltimore and Washington Railroad.   Population, 1,575.

Port Herman; town on Elk River in Cecil County.

Portobello; point in St. Mary County, projecting into St. Mary River.

Port Republic; post village in Calvert County.

Port Tobacco; creek, a small tributary of Port Tobacco River in Charles County.

Port Tobacco; post village in Charles County.

Port Tobacco; river, a tributary of Potomac River in Charles County.

Port Tobacco; station in Charles County on the Philadelphia, Baltimore and Washington Railroad.

Potomac; post village in Montgomery County.

Potomac; river, the largest in Maryland, heading in the southwestern part of the State, near Fairfax Stone, where it is known as the North Branch; thence it flows northeast as far as Cumberland, then turns to the southeast and is joined by the South Branch.   Below the junction it flows northeast as far as Hancock, and then takes a southeast course again.   At Harpers Ferry it is joined by the Shenandoah on the south and passes the Blue Ridge.   Eighteen miles above Washington are the Great Falls, and below that a succession of rapids and falls extending to the District of Columbia.   In this stretch it passes the fall line. Below Washington the course is southwest for 40 miles, when it again turns to the east and southeast and enters Chesapeake Bay at Point Lookout.   Below Washington it is tidal, has little current, and forms an estuary.   The entire drainage basin of the river is 14,479 square miles.

Potomac; station in Allegany County on the Baltimore and Ohio and the West Virginia Central and Pittsburg railroads.

Potter; creek, a small tributary of Potomac River in St. Mary County.

Powell; landing on Wye River in Talbot County.

Powellsville; post village in Wicomico County.

Powhatan; village in Baltimore County.

Pratt; post village in Allegany County.

Preston; post village in Caroline County on the Baltimore, Chesapeake and Atlantic Railway.

Prettyboy; branch, a small tributary of Gunpowder Falls in Baltimore County.

Price; creek, a small tributary of St. Mary River in St. Mary County.

Prices; post village in Queen Anne County.

Priceville; village in Baltimore County.

Prickly; point in Somerset County, projecting into Manokin River.

Priests; point in St. Mary County, projecting into St. Mary River.

Prince Fredericktown; county seat of Calvert County.

Prince George; county, organized in 1645, is bounded on the northeast and east by Patuxent River, south by Charles County, west by Potomac River, and on the northwest by the District of Columbia and Montgomery County. The surface is rolling and well supplied with springs and running streams flowing into the two bordering rivers. The area is 482 square miles, of which more than one-half, or 174,273 acres, was under cultivation in 1900. The population for the same year was 29,898. The county seat is Upper Marlboro. It contains also the towns of Hyattsville and Laurel, with populations 1,222 and 2,079 respectively. The average magnetic declination in the county in 1900 was 4° 50′ west. The annual rainfall commonly ranges between 45 and 50 inches, and the mean annual temperature between 50° and 55°.

Princess Anne; county seat of Somerset County on the New York, Philadelphia and Norfolk Railroad. Population, 857.

Principio; creek, a small tributary of Furnace Creek in Cecil County.

Principio Furnace; post village in Cecil County.

Principio Station; station in Cecil County on the Philadelphia, Baltimore and Washington Railroad.

Probasco; landing on Wye River in Talbot County.

Prospect; bay, a small arm of Eastern Bay in Queen Anne County.

Prospect; village in Harford County.

Protestant; point in St. Mary County, projecting into Breton Bay.

Providence Mill; post village in Cecil County on the Baltimore and Ohio Railroad.

Pry; cove, a small inlet of Holland Straits in South Marsh in Somerset County.

Pry; small marshy island in Holland Straits in Somerset County.

Pumphrey; village in Anne Arundel County on the Baltimore and Annopolis Short Line Railroad.

Punch; point in Talbot County, projecting into Eastern Bay.

Punch Island; creek, a small tributary of Chesapeake Bay in Dorchester County.

Pungers; small creek in South Marsh in Somerset County tributary to Holland Straits.

Purdum; post village in Montgomery County.

Purnell; bay, an arm of Chincoteague Bay in Worcester County.

Purnell; point in Worcester County, projecting into Chincoteague Bay.

Purnell; pond in Worcester County drained by Pattys Branch, a tributary of Pocomoke River.

Purnell; pond, an inlet of Chincoteague Bay in Worcester County.

Purslane; run, a small tributary of Potomac River.

Pusey; branch, a small tributary of Dividing Creek in Worcester County.

Putnam; village in Harford County.

Puzzley; run, a stream rising in Garrett County and flowing through Pennsylvania into Whites Creek.

Pylesville; post village in Harford County on the Maryland and Pennsylvania Railroad.

Quaker; neck, a strip of land lying between East Fork of Langford Bay and Chester River in Kent County.

Quaker; wharf on Chester River in Kent County.

Quantico; creek, a tributary of Nanticoke River in Wicomico County.

Queen Anne; county, organized in 1706, is situated on the eastern shore of Chesapeake Bay, extending from the Delaware State line on the east to Chesapeake Bay on the west, and is bounded on the north by Chester River and south by Talbot and Caroline counties. The surface is generally low and level, and is drained by numerous creeks. The area is 376 square miles, of which almost three-fourths, or 172,396 acres, was under cultivation in 1900. The population for the same year was 18,364. The county seat is Centerville, with a population of 1,231 inhabitants in 1900. The average magnetic declination in the county in 1900 was 5° 35′ west. The annual rainfall commonly ranges between 45 and 50 inches, and the mean annual temperature between 50° and 55°.

Queen Anne; post village in Queen Anne County on the Philadelphia, Baltimore and Washington and the Queen Anne's railroads.

Queenstown; creek, a small tributary of Chester River in Queen Anne County.

Queenstown; town in Queen Anne County on the Queen Anne's Railroad. Population, 374.

Queen Tree; landing on Patuxent River in St. Mary County.

Queponco; village in Worcester County on the Philadelphia, Baltimore and Washington Railroad.

Quince Orchard; post village in Montgomery County.

Raccoon; creek, a small tributary to Fishing Bay in Dorchester County.

Raccoon; point in Somerset County, projecting into Manokin River.

Ragged; mountain, a spur of Polish Mountain in Allegany County.

Ragged; point in Dorchester County, projecting into Little Choptank River.

Raisins; wharf on Sassafras River in Kent County.

Randallstown; post village in Baltimore County.

Randolph; post village in Montgomery County on the Baltimore and Ohio Railroad.

Raspeburg; post village in Baltimore County.

Rattlesnake; small marshy island in Chincoteague Bay in Worcester County.

Rattlesnake; landing on Chincoteague Bay in Worcester County.

Rawlings; post village in Allegany County on the Baltimore and Ohio, and the West Virginia Central and Pittsburg railroads.

Raxton; village in Baltimore County.

Rayville; village in Baltimore County.

Reason; run, a small stream rising in Garrett County and flowing through Pennsylvania into Youghiogheny River.

Reckord; post village in Baltimore County.

Red; point in Cecil County, projecting into Northeast River.

Red; outlying broken ridge west of and parallel to Meadow Mountain in Garrett County.

Red; run, a small branch of Big Piney Run in Garrett County.

Reddy; small branch of Hawlings River in Montgomery County.

Redgate; post village in St. Mary County.

Red House; branch, a small tributary of Tuckahoe Creek in Queen Anne County.

Red House; creek, a small tributary of Back River in Baltimore County.

Redhouse; post village in Garrett County.

Redland; post village in Montgomery County.

Red Lion; branch, a small tributary of Chester River in Queen Anne County.

Reed; creek, a small tributary of Chester River in Queen Anne County.

Reeder; wharf on Patuxent River in St. Mary County.

Reeds; creek, a small tributary of Choptank River in Talbot County.

Reedsgrove; post village in Somerset County.

Reedy; small marshy island in Assawoman Bay in Worcester County.

Reedy; small marshy island in Isle of Wight Bay in Worcester County.

Rehobeth; post village in Somerset County.

Reid; post village in Washington County on the Western Maryland Railroad.

Reistertown; post village in Baltimore County.

Relay; station in Baltimore County on the Baltimore and Ohio Railroad.

Renix; village in Allegany County on the Baltimore and Ohio Railroad.

Renonco; creek, a small tributary of Nanticoke River in Wicomico County.

Revell; post village in Anne Arundel County on the Baltimore and Annapolis Short Line Railroad.

Revels; neck, a strip of land lying between Kings Creek and Back River in Somerset County.

Rewastico; creek, a tributary of Nanticoke River in Wicomico County.

Reybold; wharf on Elk River in Cecil County.

Rhine; creek, a tributary of Cherry Creek in Garrett County.

Rhode; hill, a summit in Garrett County.

Rhode; river, a tributary of West River in Anne Arundel County.

Rhodesdale; post village in Dorchester County on the Baltimore, Chesapeake and Atlantic Railway.

Rich; small marshy island in Assawoman Bay in Worcester County.

Richardsmere; post village in Cecil County.

Richland; cove, a small inlet of Chesapeake Bay in Dorchester County.

Richland; point in Dorchester County, projecting into Chesapeake Bay.

Rick; neck, a strip of land between Elk and Sassafras rivers in Cecil County.

Rickett; point in Harford County, projecting into Gunpowder River.

Ricks; point in Worcester County, projecting into Chincoteague Bay.

Rider; post village in Baltimore County.

Ridge; post village in St. Mary County.

Ridgely; post village in Caroline County on the Philadelphia, Baltimore and Washington Railroad.

Ridgeville; village in Carroll County.

Ridgley; cove, a small inlet of Middle Branch of Patapsco River within chartered limits of Baltimore City.

Ridgley; hill, a summit in Garrett County. Height, 2,617 feet.

Ridout; creek, a small tributary of Whitehall River in Anne Arundel County.

Riggs Mills; village in Prince George County.

Rioll; cove, a small inlet of Little Choptank River in Dorchester County.

Riley; cove, a small inlet of Chincoteague Bay in Worcester County.

Ripley; post village in Charles County.

Rising Sun; post village in Cecil County on the Philadelphia, Baltimore and Washington Railroad. Population, 382.

Ritchie; post village in Prince George County on the Chesapeake Beach Railway.

River; hill, a summit in Garrett County. Elevation, 2,700 feet.

Riverdale; post village in Prince George County on the Baltimore and Ohio Railroad.

Riverside; post village in Charles County.

Riverside; village in Talbot County on the Baltimore, Chesapeake and Atlantic Railway.

River Springs; post village in St. Mary County.
Riverton; post village in Wicomico County.
Riverview; post village in Anne Arundel County.
River View; village in Prince George County.
Rives; village in Prince George County.
Roach; point in Cecil County, projecting into Northeast River.
Roaring; point in Wicomico County, projecting into Nanticoke River.
Roberts; small island in Susquehanna River in Harford County.
Roberts; post village in Queen Anne County.
Roberts; village in Allegany County on the Baltimore and Ohio Railroad.
Robin; a small inlet of Chester River in Queen Anne County.
Robin; point in Harford County, projecting into Chesapeake Bay.
Robins; branch, a small tributary of Choptank River in Caroline County.
Robins; creek, a small tributary to Chincoteague Bay in Worcester County.
Robins; marsh in Chincoteague Bay in Worcester County.
Robinson; neck, a strip of land between Beaverdam and St. John creeks in Dorchester County.
Robinson; post village in Anne Arundel County on the Baltimore and Annapolis Short Line Railroad.
Rock; creek, a small branch of Carroll Creek in Frederick County.
Rock; creek, a small tributary to Chesapeake Bay in Somerset County.
Rock; creek, a small tributary of Potomac River in Montgomery County.
Rock; creek, a small tributary of Patuxent River in Calvert County.
Rock; creek, a small tributary of Tangier Sound in Somerset County.
Rock; creek, a small tributary of Patuxent River in Prince George County.
Rock; creek, a small tributary of Patapsco River in Anne Arundel County.
Rock; hole, a small inlet of Tangier Sound in Somerset County.
Rock; point in Anne Arundel County, projecting into Patapsco River.
Rock; point in Charles County, projecting into Wicomico River.
Rock; run, a small branch of Buffalo Creek in Garrett County.
Rock; run, a small tributary of Susquehanna River in Cecil County.
Rock; run, a small tributary of Susquehanna River in Harford County.
Rockawalking; creek, a tributary of Wicomico River in Wicomico County.
Rockawalking; post village in Wicomico County.
Rockburn; branch, a small tributary of Patapsco River in Howard County.
Rockdale; village in Baltimore County.
Rock Gully; creek, a small branch of Evitts Creek in Allegany County.
Rockhall; creek, a small tributary to Chesapeake Bay in Kent County.
Rockhall; landing on Chesapeake Bay in Kent County.
Rockhall; post village in Kent County.
Rockland; village in Baltimore County on the Northern Central Railway.
Rockpoint; post village in Charles County.
Rock Run; village in Cecil County on the Philadelphia, Baltimore and Washington Railroad.
Rocks; post village in Harford County.
Rocksprings; post village in Cecil County.
Rockville; county seat of Montgomery County on the Baltimore and Ohio Railroad. Population, 1,110.
Rocky; branch, a small tributary of Little Gunpowder Falls in Harford County.
Rocky; point in Baltimore County, projecting into Back River.
Rocky; point in Cecil County, projecting into Chesapeake Bay.
Rockyridge; post village in Frederick County on the Emmitsburg and the Western Maryland railroads.
Roe; post village in Queen Anne County

Rogers; village in Baltimore County on the Northern Central Railway.

Rogue Harbor; branch, a small tributary of Little Patuxent River in Anne Arundel County.

Rogues; harbor, a small inlet of Elk River in Cecil County.

Rohrersville; post village in Washington County on the Baltimore and Ohio Railroad.

Rollin; village in Calvert County.

Rolphs; post village in Queen Anne County.

Roman; nose, a mountain ridge in Garrett County.   Elevation, 3,006 feet.

Romney; creek, a small tributary to Chesapeake Bay in Harford County.

Rosaryville; post village in Prince George County.

Rosecroft; post village in Prince George County.

Rosedale; village in Baltimore County on the Baltimore and Ohio Railroad.

Rose Neck; point in Dorchester County, projecting into Fishing Bay.

Roslyn; post village in Baltimore County.

Ross; small island in Susquehanna River in Harford County.

Rossville; post village in Baltimore County on the Baltimore and Ohio Railroad.

Rosten; creek, a small tributary of Chester River in Queen Anne County.

Rough; small island in Susquehanna River in Cecil County.

Round; bay, a small inlet of Severn River in Anne Arundel County.

Round Glade; run, a small tributary of Youghiogheny River in Garrett County.

Round Bay; village in Anne Arundel County on the Baltimore and Annapolis Short Line Railroad.

Roundtop; hill, a summit in Tonoloway Ridge.   Elevation, 1,388 feet.

Roundtop; wharf on Chester River in Kent County.

Rover; post village in Howard County.

Rowie; village in Prince George County.

Rowland; small island in Susquehanna River in Harford County.

Rowlandsville; post village in Cecil County on the Philadelphia, Baltimore and Washington Railroad.

Rowley; cove, an inlet of Chincoteague Bay in Worcester County.

Roxbury; post village in Washington County on the Baltimore and Ohio Railroad.

Roxbury Mills; post village in Howard County.

Royal Oak; post village in Talbot County on the Baltimore, Chesapeake and Atlantic Railway.

Royal Oak; village in Wicomico County on the Baltimore, Chesapeake and Atlantic Railway.

Royston; small island at mouth of Broad Creek in Talbot County.

Ruhl; village in Baltimore County.

Rush; village in Allegany County.

Rush; post village in Allegany County.

Rushville; village in Montgomery County.

Russell; branch, a small tributary of Dry Seneca Creek in Montgomery Courty.

Ruthsburg; post village in Queen Anne County.

Rutland; post village in Anne Arundel County.

Rutledge; post village in Harford County.

Ryceville; post village in Charles County.

Sabellasville; post village in Frederick County on the Western Maryland Railroad.

Sackertown; village in Somerset County.

St. Augustine; post village in Cecil County.

St. Catherine; small island in Potomac River in St. Mary County.

St. Catherine; small island in Susquehanna River in Harford County.

St. Catherine; sound, a small inlet of Potomac River in St. Mary County

St. Clement; bay, an inlet of Potomac River in St. Mary County.

St. Clement; creek, a tributary to St. Clement Bay in St. Mary County.

St. Clement Bay; village in St. Mary County.

St. George; creek, a small tributary of Potomac River in St. Mary County.

St. George; island in Potomac River in St. Mary County.

St. George; post village in Baltimore County.

St. George Island; post village in St. Mary County.

St. Helena; small island in Round Bay in Anne Arundel County.

St. Inigoes; creek, a small tributary of St. Mary River in St. Mary County.

St. Inigoes; post village in St. Mary County.

St. James Corners; village in Baltimore County.

St. James School; post village in Washington County.

St. Jerome; creek, a small tributary to Chesapeake Bay in St. Mary County.

St. Jerome; point in St. Mary County, projecting into Chesapeake Bay.

St. John; creek, a small tributary of Patuxent River in Calvert County.

St. John; creek, a small tributary of Punch Island Creek in Dorchester County.

St. John; creek, a small tributary of Patuxent River in St. Mary County.

St. John; rock, a summit on Big Savage Mountain. Elevation, 2,930 feet.

St. Leonard; creek, a small tributary of Patuxent River in Calvert County.

St. Leonard; post village in Calvert County.

St. Margaret; small island in Wicomico River in St. Mary County.

St. Margaret; village in Anne Arundel County.

St. Martin; post village in Worcester County on the Baltimore, Chesapeake and Atlantic Railway.

St. Mary; county, settled in 1634, occupies the southeast extremity of the western shore of the Chesapeake Bay, and forms a peninsula bounded on the southwest by Potomac River, on the northeast by the bay and Patuxent River, and northwest by Charles County. The surface of the county is varied, the northwestern portion being undulated, while the southeastern portion is mostly level and low. It is well drained by numerous creeks and branches. The area is 372 square miles, of which nearly one-half, or 109,553 acres, was under cultivation in 1900. The population for the same year was 17,182. The county seat is Leonardtown. The average magnetic declination in the county in 1900 was 4° 30′. The annual rainfall commonly ranges between 45 and 50 inches, and the mean annual temperature between 55° and 60°.

St. Mary; post village in St. Mary County.

St. Mary; river, an estuary flowing into Potomac River near its mouth.

St. Michaels; post village in Talbot County on the Baltimore, Chesapeake and Atlantic Railway. Population, 1,043.

St. Patrick; creek, a small tributary to St. Clement Bay in St. Mary County.

St. Peters; creek, a small tributary of Manokin River in Somerset County.

St. Pierre; small marshy island in Manokin River in Somerset County.

St. Pierre; point in Somerset County, projecting into Manokin River.

St. Stephen; village in Somerset County.

Salem; post village in Dorchester County.

Salisbury; county seat of Wicomico County on the Baltimore, Chesapeake and Atlantic and the New York, Philadelphia and Norfolk railroads. Population, 4,277.

Salt Block; mountain in Garrett County. Elevation, 2,768 feet.

Saltblock; run, a small tributary of Youghiogheny River in Garrett County.

Saltgrass; point in Worcester County, projecting into St. Martin River.

Saltpeter; creek, a small tributary of Bush River in Baltimore County.

Sampson; rock, a summit in Big Savage Mountain. Elevation, 2,942 feet.

Sams; creek, a small tributary of Piney Branch in Carroll County.

Sand; run, a tributary of North Branch of Potomac River in Garrett County.

Sandgates; post village in St. Mary County.

Sandy; branch, a small tributary of Potomac River in Montgomery County.

Sandy; point in Anne Arundel County, projecting into Chesapeake Bay.

Sandy; point in Calvert County, projecting into Patuxent River.

Sandy; point in Harford County, projecting into Bush River.

Sandy; point in Harford County, projecting into Chesapeake Bay.

Sandy; point in Worcester County, projecting into Chincoteague Bay.

Sandy; point in Worcester County, projecting into Sinepuxent Bay.

Sandy Bottom; village in Kent County.

Sandy Hill; landing on Nanticoke River in Wicomico County.

Sandy Hook; village in Washington County on the Baltimore and Ohio Railroad.

Sandy Point; small marshy island in Sinepuxent Bay in Worcester County.

Sandyspring; post village in Montgomery County.

Sang; run, a small tributary of Youghiogheny River in Garrett County.

Sang Run; post village in Garrett County.

Sassafras; post village in Kent County.

Sassafras; neck, a strip of land lying between Sassafras and Bohemia rivers in Cecil County.

Sassafras; river on boundary between Cecil and Kent counties, a tributary to Chesapeake Bay.

Saunders; point in Anne Arundel County, projecting into Chesapeake Bay.

Savage; post village in Howard County on the Baltimore and Ohio Railroad.

Savage; river, tributary of North Branch of Potomac River in Garrett County.

Savannah; small lake drained by Jack Creek, a tributary of Nanticoke River in Dorchester County.

Saw Mill; branch, a small tributary of Furnace Creek in Anne Arundel County.

Sawmill; branch, a small tributary of Little Gunpowder Falls in Baltimore County.

Sawmill; creek, a small tributary of Sassafras River in Kent County.

Sawney; cove, a small inlet of Chesapeake Bay in Somerset County.

Sawpit; run, a small tributary of Town Creek in Allegany County.

Scaffold; creek, a small tributary of West River in Anne Arundel County.

Scaggsville; post village in Howard County.

Scarboro; creek, a small tributary to Chincoteague Bay in Worcester County.

Scarboro; post village in Harford County on the Philadelphia, Baltimore and Washington Railroad.

Scarff; post village in Harford County.

Schoolhouse; hill in Harford County.

Schoolhouse; run, a small tributary of Castleman River in Garrett County.

Scotchman; creek, a small tributary of Bohemia River in Cecil County.

Scotland; post village in St. Mary County.

Scott; point in Somerset County, projecting into Big Annemessex River.

Scott Level; village in Baltimore County.

Scotts; landing on Chincoteague Bay in Worcester County.

Seabrook; post village in Prince George County on the Philadelphia, Baltimore and Washington Railroad.

Seat Pleasant; post village in Prince George County.

Sea Wall Junction; village in Anne Arundel County on the Baltimore and Ohio Railroad.

Second; creek, a small tributary of Patuxent River in St. Mary County.

Second Mine; branch, a small tribuary of Gunpowder Falls in Baltimore County.

Secretary; creek, a small tributary of Choptank River in Dorchester County.

Secretary; village in Dorchester County. Population, 410.

Selby; bay, a small inlet at mouth of South River in Anne Arundel County.

Selbysport; post village in Garrett County on the Baltimore and Ohio Railroad.

Sellman; post village in Montgomery County.

Seneca; creek, a small tributary to Chesapeake Bay in Baltimore County.

Seneca; point in Cecil County, projecting into Northeast River.

Seneca; post village in Montgomery County.

Severn; post village in Anne Arundel County on the Philadelphia, Baltimore and Washington Railroad.

Severn; river in Anne Arundel County flowing into Chesapeake Bay.

Severn; run, a small tributary of Severn River in Anne Arundel County.

Sewell; post village in Harford County on the Baltimore and Ohio Railroad.

Shad; point in Wicomico County, projecting into Wicomico River.

Shadow Hall; point in Cecil County, projecting into Furnace Creek.

Shadyside; post village in Anne Arundel County.

Shaft; post village in Allegany County.

Shallow; creek, a small tributary of Patapsco River in Baltimore County.

Shamburg; village in Baltimore County.

Shane; post village in Baltimore County.

Sharon; post village in Harford County on the Maryland and Pennsylvania Railroad.

Sharperville; village in Prince George County.

Sharps; small island in Chesapeake Bay in Dorchester County.

Sharps; point in Wicomico County, projecting into Wicomico River.

Sharpsburg; town in Washington County. Population, 1,030.

Sharptown; town in Wicomico County. Population, 529.

Shaw; bay, a small inlet of Eastern Bay in Talbot County.

Shawan; village in Baltimore County.

Shawsville; village in Harford County.

Sheepshead; harbor, an inlet of Kedge Straits in Somerset County.

Shellcorn; wharf on Sassafras River in Kent County.

Shelltown; post village in Somerset County.

Sheppard; post village in Baltimore County on the Maryland and Pennsylvania Railroad.

Sheridan; point in Calvert County, projecting into Patuxent River.

Sheridan Point; post village in Calvert County.

Sherwood; village in Baltimore County on the Northern Central Railway.

Sherwood; post village in Talbot County.

Shields; run, a small tributary of North Branch of Potomac River in Garrett County.

Shingle; landing on Shingle Landing Prong in Worcester County.

Shingle Landing; prong, a small tributary of St. Martin River in Worcester County.

Ship; cove, a small inlet of Chester River in Kent County.

Shipley; point in Cecil County, projecting into Furnace Creek.

Shipley; village in Anne Arundel County on the Baltimore and Annapolis Short Line Railroad.

Shipping; creek, a small tributary to Eastern Bay in Queen Anne County.

Shipping; point in St. Mary County, projecting into St. Clement Bay.

Shirtpond; cove, a small inlet at mouth of Big Annemessex River in Somerset County.

Shoal; creek, a small tributary of Choptank River in Dorchester County.

Shock Mills; village in Carroll County.

Short; point in St. Mary County, projecting into St. Martin River.

Shorters; landing on Backgarden Creek in Dorchester County.

Short Line; junction, a station in Harford County on the Baltimore and Annapolis Short Line and the Bay Ridge railroads.

Showell; post village in Worcester County on the Philadelphia, Baltimore and Washington Railroad.

Shrewsbury; neck, a strip of land lying between Turner and Freeman creeks in Kent County.

Shriver; ridge, a continuation of Knobby Mountain of West Virginia separating two small branches of North Branch of Potomac River.

Shures Landing; post village in Harford County.

Sickle; hill on boundary between West Virginia and Garrett County. Elevation, 2,400 feet.

Sideling; hill, a mountain ridge in Washington County extending into Pennsylvania.

Sideling Hill; creek, a tributary of Potomac River on boundary between Allegany and Washington counties.

Siebert; post village in Allegany County.

Silesia; post village in Prince George County.

Silver; run, a small tributary of Big Pipe Creek in Carroll County.

Silverhill; post village in Prince George County.

Silver Spring; post village in Montgomery County on the Baltimore and Ohio Railroad.

Simpsonville; post village in Howard County.

Sinepuxent; neck, a strip of land lying between Sinepuxent and Newport bays in Worcester County.

Sinepuxent; village in Worcester County on the Philadelphia, Baltimore and Washington Railroad.

Sines; post village in Garrett County.

Singer; post village in Harford County.

Singerly; post village and station in Cecil County on the Baltimore and Ohio Railroad.

Skipnish; village in Garrett County on the Baltimore and Ohio Railroad.

Skipper; creek, a small tributary of Chester River in Kent County.

Skipton; creek, a small tributary of Wye River in Talbot County.

Skipton; post village in Talbot County.

Sledds; point in Anne Arundel County, projecting into Curtis Bay.

Slidell; post village in Montgomery County.

Sligo; post village in Montgomery County.

Sligo; small branch of Northwest Branch in Prince George County.

Smith; cove, a small inlet of Choptank River in Dorchester County.

Smith; cove, a small inlet of Middle Branch of Patapsco River within limits of Baltimore city.

Smith; creek, a small tributary of Potomac River in St. Mary County.

Smith; small island in Chesapeake Bay in Somerset County.

Smith; point in Talbot County, projecting into Harris Creek.

Smithsburg; town in Washington County.   Population, 462.

Smithville; post village in Caroline County.

Smithville; village in Dorchester County.

Smithville; village in Kent County.

Smokehouse; cove, a small inlet of St. Martin River in Worcester County.

Snaggy; hill in Garrett County.

Snake; small island in Susquehanna River in Harford County.

Snow Hill; county seat of Worcester County on the Philadelphia, Baltimore and Washington Railroad.   Population, 1,596.

Snowy; creek, a small branch of Youghiogheny River in Garrett County.

Sollers; point in Baltimore County, projecting into Patapsco River.

Sollers; post village in Calvert County on the Northern Central Railway.

Solley; post village in Anne Arundel County.

Solomon; ridge, a spur of Meadow Mountain separating Dry and Big runs in Garrett County.

Solomons; post village in Calvert County.

Solomons Lump; small island in Kedge Straits in Somerset County.   A light-house is erected thereon.

Somerset; county, is the southernmost bay county of the Eastern Shore.   It is bounded on the north by Wicomico County, east by Worcester County, south by Pocomoke River and Sound, and west by Chesapeake Bay.   The surface is generally level, but sufficiently undulating to afford good drainage.   The area is 362 square miles, of which more than a third, or 82,650 acres, was under cultivation in 1900.   The population for the same year was 25,193.   The county seat is Princess Anne.   It also contains the town of Crisfield, of 3,165 inhabitants in 1900.   The average magnetic declination in the county in 1900 was 5° 00′.   The annual rainfall commonly ranges between 45 and 50 inches, and the mean annual temperature between 55° and 60°.

Somerset; creek, a small tributary of Wicomico Creek in Somerset County.

Sopers; creek, a small branch of Little Bennetts Creek in Montgomery County.

Sopers; hill in Montgomery County.   Elevation, 469.

Sotterly; point in St. Mary County, projecting into Patuxent River.

Sotterly; post village in St. Mary County.

South; branch, a tributary of Bear Creek in Garrett County.

South; branch, a tributary of Shingle Landing Prong in Worcester County.

South; branch, a tributary of Castleman River in Garrett County.

South; branch, a tributary of Laurel Run in Garrett County.

South; fork, a branch of Linganore Creek in Frederick County.

South; fork, a tributary of Bens Creek in Frederick County.

South; fork, a tributary of Green Run in Wicomico County.

South; fork, a tributary of Sand Run in Garrett County.

South; hammock, small bits of marshy land in Assawoman Bay in Worcester County.

South; large marshy island in Somerset County between Holland and Kedge straits.

South; river in Anne Arundel County flowing into Chesapeake Bay.

South Branch of Patapsco; river, on boundary between Howard and Carroll counties.

South Cumberland; village in Allegany County.

Southeast; creek, a small tributary of Chester River in Queen Anne County.

South River; post village in Anne Arundel County.

South Tuscarora; creek, a small tributary of Potomac River in Frederick County.

Southwest; small branch of Western Branch in Prince George County.

Spaniards; neck, a strip of land lying between Chester and Corsica rivers in Queen Anne County.

Sparks; village in Baltimore County on the Northern Central Railway.

Sparrow; point in Baltimore County, projecting into Patapsco River.

Sparrow Point; town in Baltimore County on the Northern Central Railway.

Spaw; creek, a small tributary to Annapolis Roads in Anne Arundel County.

Spedden; wharf on Hudson Creek in Dorchester County.

Speelman Mills; village in Garrett County.

Spence; cove, small inlet of Newport Bay in Worcester County.

Spence; post village in Worcester County.

Spencer; creek, a small tributary of Edge Creek in Talbot County.

Spencer; creek, a small tributary of Miles River in Talbot County.

Spencer; small island in Susquehanna River in Harford County.

Spencers; wharf on Town Creek in St. Mary County.

Spencerville; post village in Montgomery County.

Spesutie; large, almost entirely marshy island in Chesapeake Bay in Harford County.

Spesutie; narrows, a passageway separating Spesutie Island from the mainland in Harford County.

Spielman; post village in Washington County.

Spiker; run, a small tributary of Castleman River in Garrett County.

Spook; hill in Baltimore County.

Spring; creek, a small tributary of Choptank River in Caroline County.

Spring; creek, a small tributary of Patuxent River in St. Mary County.

Spring; small marshy island in Holland Straits in Dorchester County.

Springfield; post village in Prince George County on the Philadelphia, Baltimore and Washington Railroad.

Springhill; post village in Charles County.

Springlick; run, a small tributary of Crabtree Creek in Garrett County.

Spry; small marshy island at mouth of Gunpowder River in Harford County.

Squirrel Neck; run, a small tributary of Georges Creek in Allegany County.

Stabler; hill in Montgomery County. Elevation, 571 feet.

Stablersville; village in Baltimore County.

Stafford; post village in Harford County.

Stanley; run, a small tributary of Swanson Creek in Prince George County.

Stansberry; point in Baltimore County, projecting into Back River.

Starkley Corner; village in Queen Anne County.

Staub; run, a small tributary of Georges Creek in Allegany County.

Steele; small island in Susquehanna River in Cecil County.

Stemmer; run, a small branch of Northeast Creek in Baltimore County.

Stephensville; post village in Queen Anne County.

Stepney; post village in Harford County on the Baltimore and Ohio Railroad.

Sterrer; small island in Susquehanna River in Cecil County.

Stevenson; post village in Baltimore County on the Northern Central Railway.

Steves Island; village in Worcester County.

Stewart; neck, a strip of land lying between Kings and Jones creeks and Manokin River in Somerset County.

Still; small pond at junction of Churn and Stillpond creeks in Kent County.

Stillpond; creek, a small tributary to Still Pond in Kent County.

Stillpond; post village in Kent County on the Philadelphia, Baltimore and Washington Railroad.

Stirrup; run, a small branch of Deer Creek in Harford County.

Stockton; town in Worcester County.

Stoddart; point in Charles County, projecting into Wicomico River.

Stone; point in Harford County, projecting into Chesapeake Bay.

Stone; run, a small branch of Octararo Creek in Cecil County.

Stone; wharf on St. Clement Bay in St. Mary County.

Stone House; cove, a small inlet of Curtis Bay in Anne Arundel County.

Stony; run, a small tributary of Patapsco River in Anne Arundel County.

Stony; run, a small branch of Northeast River in Cecil County.

Stony; run, a small branch of North Branch of Potomac River in Garrett County.

Stony; creek, a tributary of Patapsco River in Anne Arundel County.

Stony; creek, a tributary of Monocacy River in Frederick County.

Stony; point in Anne Arundel County, projecting into Patapsco River.

Stony; point in Cecil County, projecting into Elk River.

Stony Run; station in Anne Arundel County on the Philadelphia, Baltimore and Washington Railroad.

Stratford; small mountain ridge in Allegany County lying between Sawpit Run and Town Creek.

Strawberry; creek, a small tributary of Middle River in Baltimore County.
Street; post village in Harford County.
Striking; marshy bit of land in Worcester County in Chincoteague Bay.
Stringtown; village in Baltimore County.
Stump; small island in Susquehanna River in Harford County.
Stump; point in Cecil County, projecting into Chesapeake Bay.
Sturges; creek, a small branch of Nassawango Creek in Worcester County.
Sudbrook Park; post village in Baltimore County.
Sudlersville; post village in Queen Anne County on the Philadelphia, Baltimore and Washington Railroad.
Sudley; post village in Anne Arundel County.
Sue; creek, a small tributary of Middle River in Baltimore County.
Sue; point in Baltimore County, projecting into Middle River.
Sugar; point in Worcester County, projecting into Choptank River.
Sugar Hill; village in Harford County.
Sugarland; post village in Montgomery County.
Sugar Loaf; mountain, a hill in Montgomery County.   Elevation, 1,281 feet.
Suitland; village in Prince George County.
Sumiac; pond in Wicomico County drained by Beaverdam Creek, a tributary of Wicomico River.
Summerfield; village in Baltimore County on the Maryland and Pennsylvania Railroad.
Summerville; village in Calvert County.
Sunderland; post village in Calvert County.
Sunnybrook; post village in Baltimore County.
Sunnyside; post village in Garrett County.
Sunnyside; village in Prince George County on Baltimore and Ohio Railroad.
Susquehanna; neck, a strip of land lying between Slaughter and Woolford creeks in Dorchester County.
Swallow; falls in Youghiogheny River in Garrett County.
Swamp; run, a small tributary of Little Swamp River in Garrett County.
Swan; creek, a small tributary of Patapsco River in Anne Arundel County.
Swan; creek, a small tributary to Chesapeake Bay in Harford County.
Swan; creek, a tributary of Sassafras River in Kent County.
Swan; small island in Chesapeake Bay in Dorchester County.
Swan; small marshy island in Chesapeake Bay in Somerset County.
Swan; gut, a small branch of Greys Creek in Worcester County.
Swan; point in Charles County, projecting into Potomac River.
Swan; point in Kent County, projecting into Chesapeake Bay.
Swan Creek; village in Harford County on the Baltimore and Ohio and the Philadelphia, Baltimore and Washington railroads.
Swanson; creek, a small tributary of Patuxent River on boundary between Prince George and Charles counties.
Swanton; post village in Garrett County on the Baltimore and Ohio Railroad.
Sweetair; post village in Baltimore County.
Sykesville; post village in Carroll County on the Baltimore and Ohio Railroad.
Sylmar; post village in Cecil County on the Philadelphia, Baltimore and Washington Railroad.
Table; rock, a summit in Backbone Mountain in Garrett County.
Takoma; town in Montgomery County on the Baltimore and Ohio Railroad.   Population, 756.
Talbert; village in Prince George County on the Philadelphia, Baltimore and Washington Railroad.
Talbot; branch, a small tributary of Linganore Creek in Frederick County.

Talbot; county, bounded southerly and southeasterly by the Choptank River and Tuckahoe Creek, northerly by Queen Anne County, and westerly by Chesapeake Bay. The surface is generally low and level and well drained by numerous streams flowing into the bay and bordering rivers. The area is 286 square miles, almost two-thirds of which, or 119,266 acres, were under cultivation in 1900. The population for the same year was 20,342. The county seat is Easton with a population of 3,074. St. Michaels and Oxford are also in this county and have a population of 1,042 and 1,243, respectively. The average magnetic declination in the county in 1900 was 5° 25' west. The annual rainfall commonly ranges between 45 and 50 inches and the mean annual temperature between 50° and 55°.

Tally; point in Anne Arundel County, projecting into Chesapeake Bay.

Taneytown; town in Carroll County. Population 665.

Tangier; sound, a part of Chesapeake Bay inclosed between series of low, marshy islands and the mainland of the peninsula in Somerset County.

Tanhouse; creek, a small tributary to Chincoteague Bay in Worcester County.

Tanner; creek, a small tributary to Chesapeake Bay in St. Mary County.

Tannery; post village in Carroll County.

Tanyard; post village in Caroline County.

Tar; bay, a small inlet of Chesapeake Bay in Dorchester County.

Tar Coal; cove, a small inlet of Magothy River, in Anne Arundel County.

Tarkiln; run, a small tributary of Castleman River in Garrett County.

Tars; creek, a small tributary of Tred Avon River in Talbot County.

Tasker Corners; village in Garrett County.

Tate; landing on Deep Creek in Anne Arundel County.

Tavern; creek, a small tributary to Chesapeake Bay.

Taylor; island, a large strip of elevated dry land in sea marshes of Dorchester County.

Taylor; landing on Chincoteague Bay in Worcester County.

Taylor; point in Dorchester County, projecting into Honga River.

Taylor; post village in Harford County.

Taylor Island; post village in Dorchester County.

Taylorsville; village in Carroll County.

Taylorville; village in Worcester County.

T. B.; post village in Prince George County.

Teague; creek, a small tributary of Manokin River in Somerset County.

Tedious; creek, a small tributary to Fishing Bay in Dorchester County.

Templeville; post village in Queen Anne County.

Ten Mile; creek, a small tributary of Little Seneca Creek in Montgomery County.

Terrapin Sand; cove, a small inlet of Chesapeake Bay in Somerset County.

Terrapin Sand; point in Somerset County, projecting into Chesapeake Bay.

Texas; post village in Baltimore County on the Northern Central Railway.

Thackery; point in Cecil County, projecting into Elk River.

Thayerville; post village in Garrett County.

Theodore; village in Cecil County.

The Three Sisters; three small marshy islands in Chesapeake Bay in Anne Arundel County.

Third Mine; branch, a small tributary of Gunpowder Falls in Baltimore County.

Thomas; branch, a small tributary of Patuxent River in Anne Arundel County.

Thomas; point in Anne Arundel County, projecting into Chesapeake Bay.

Thomas; post village in Dorchester County.

Thomas; run, a small branch of Cabin John Creek in Montgomery County.

Thomas; run, a small tributary of Deer Creek in Harford County.

Thomas Run; post village in Harford County.

Thompson; creek, a small branch of Cox Creek in Queen Anne County.

Thompson; village in Dorchester County on the Philadelphia, Baltimore and Washington Railroad.

Thornton; small branch of Little Gunpowder Falls in Harford County.

Thorofare; small passage between Gab Island and another small island in Somerset County.

Three Fork; run, a small tributary of North Branch of Potomac River in Garrett County.

Thrift; post village in Prince George County.

Thurmont; town in Frederick County on the Western Maryland Railroad. Population, 868.

Tilghman; cove, a small inlet of Chester River in Queen Anne County.

Tilghman; creek, a small tributary to Eastern Bay in Talbot County.

Tilghman; creek, a small tributary of Chester River in Queen Anne County.

Tilghman; small island in Talbot County separated from the mainland by Knapp Narrows.

Tilghman; point in Talbot County, projecting into Eastern Bay.

Tilghman; pond in Worcester County drained by a small branch of Pocomoke River.

Tilghman; post village in Talbot County on the Philadelphia, Baltimore and Washington Railroad.

Tingles; small marshy island in Chincoteague Bay in Worcester County.

Tinkers; creek, a small tributary of Piscataway Creek in Prince George County.

Timber; neck, a strip of land in Cecil County lying between Chesapeake Bay and Elk River.

Timber; ridge, a small mountain ridge in Washington County extending into Pennsylvania.

Timmonstown; branch, a small tributary of Pocomoke River in Worcester County.

Timonium; post village in Baltimore County on the Northern Central Railway.

Timothy; branch, a small tributary of Mattawoman Creek in Prince George County.

Tippett; post village in Prince George County.

Tizzard; small, almost entirely marshy island in Chincoteague Bay in Worcester County.

Tobacco; run, a small tributary of Deer Creek in Harford County.

Tobin; village in Baltimore County.

Todd; point in Dorchester County, projecting into Choptank River.

Toddville; post village in Dorchester County.

Tolchester Beach; post village in Kent County.

Toliver; run, a small tributary of Youghiogheny River in Garrett County.

Tolson; creek, a small tributary to Chesapeake Bay in Queen Anne County.

Tom; cove, a small inlet of Chesapeake Bay in Dorchester County.

Tom; point in Cecil County, projecting into Elk River.

Tom; ridge, a spur of Meadow Mountain extending into a bend of Middle Fork Creek in Garrett County.

Tomakokin; creek, a small tributary to St. Clement Bay in St. Mary County.

Tompkinsville; post village in Charles County.

Toms Lick; run, a small tributary of Little Youghiogheny River in Garrett County.

Tonoloway; creek, a tributary of Potomac River in Washington County.

Tonoloway; ridge, a continuation of Tonoloway Mountain Ridge of West Virginia into Washington County.

Tonytank; creek, a tributary of Wicomico River in Wicomico County.

Toulson; post village in Caroline County.

Town; creek, a small tributary of Tred Avon River in Talbot County.

Town; creek, a small tributary of Patuxent River in St. Mary County.

Town; creek, a tributary of Potomac River in Allegany County.

Town; hill, a long mountain ridge in Allegany County.

Town; point in Cecil County, projecting into Elk River.

Town; point in Charles County, projecting into Patuxent River.

Town; point in Dorchester County, projecting into Choptank River.

Town; point in St. Mary County, projecting into Patuxent River.

Towncreek; post village in Allegany County.

Town Point; neck, a strip of land lying between Bohemia and Elk rivers in Cecil County.

Townpoint; post village in Cecil County.

Townshend; post village in Prince George County.

Towsers; branch, a tributary of Little Patuxent River in Anne Arundel County.

Towson; county seat of Baltimore County on the Maryland and Pennsylvania Railroad.

Tracys Landing; post village in Anne Arundel County.

Transquaking; river in Dorchester County flowing into Fishing Bay.

Trap; run, a small tributary of Youghiogheny River in Garrett County.

Trap; village in St. Mary County.

Trappe; creek, a small tributary to Newport Bay in Worcester County.

Trappe; landing on Trappe River in Talbot County.

Trappe; river in Talbot County flowing into Choptank River.

Trappe; village in Talbot County on the Philadelphia, Baltimore and Washington Railroad. Population, 279.

Trappe; village in Wicomico County.

Travers; wharf on Le Compte Bay in Dorchester County.

Travilah; post village in Montgomery County.

Tred Avon; river, a tributary to Choptank River in Talbot County.

Trego; post village in Washington County.

Trent Hall; creek, a small tributary of Patuxent River in St. Mary County.

Triadelphia; post village in Howard County.

Trills Corner; village in Somerset County.

Trippe; bay, a small inlet of Choptank River in Dorchester County.

Trippe; creek, a tributary of Tred Avon River in Talbot County.

Trout; run, a small tributary of Little Youghiogheny River in Garrett County.

Troy; small marshy island in Chesapeake Bay in Somerset County.

Troy; village in Charles County.

Troyer; village in Baltimore County.

Trueman; point in Prince George County, projecting into Patuxent River.

Truesdell; heights, a summit in Backbone Mountain in Garrett County. Elevation, 2,809 feet.

Truitt; village in Wicomico County.

Trump; village in Baltimore County.

Tub Mill; creek, a small tributary of Choptank River in Caroline County.

Tuckahoe; creek, a tributary of Choptank River on boundary between Queen Anne, Caroline, and Talbot counties.

Tuckahoe; post village in Caroline County on the Queen Anne's Railroad.

Tull; point in Somerset County, projecting into Wicomico River.

Tulls Corner; post village in Somerset County.

Tunis Mills; post village in Talbot County.

Turkey; small branch of Western Branch in Prince George County.

Turkey; point in Anne Arundel County, projecting into South River.

Turkey; point in Baltimore County, projecting into Middle Creek.

Turkey; point in Cecil County, projecting into Chesapeake Bay.

Turkey; point in Queen Anne County, projecting into Eastern Bay.

Turkey; run, a small branch of Stony Creek in Frederick County.

Turkey Lodge; hill, a ridge lying between Elk Lick and Poplar Lick runs in Garrett County.

Turkey Neck; point in Talbot County, projecting into Harris Creek.

Turner; creek, a tributary of Sassafras River in Kent County.

Turner; gap in Blue Ridge Mountains in Frederick County.

Turner; village in St. Mary County on the Baltimore, Chesapeake and Atlantic Railway.

Turner Creek; wharf in Kent County on Turner Creek.

Turpin; cove, a small inlet of Chincoteague Bay in Worcester County.

Turtle Egg; small marshy island in Holland Straits in Somerset County.

Turville; creek, a small stream in Worcester County flowing into Isle of Wight Bay.

Tuscarora; post village in Frederick County on the Baltimore and Ohio Railroad.

Tuxedo; post village in Prince George County.

Twiggtown; post village in Allegany County.

Twilley; village in Wicomico County.

Twitch; cove, a small inlet of Tangier Sound in Somerset County.

Two Johns; post village in Caroline County.

Twomile; run, a small branch of Big Piney Run in Garrett County.

Tyaskin; post village in Wicomico County.

Uncle; village in St. Mary County.

Unicorn; branch, a small tributary of Chester River in Queen Anne County.

Union; run, a small tributary of Bush River in Harford County.

Union Bridge; town in Carroll County on the Western Maryland Railroad. Population, 663.

Unionville; village in Frederick County.

Unionville; village in Talbot County.

Unionville; village in Worcester County.

Unity; post village in Montgomery County.

Upperco; post village in Baltimore County.

Upper Crossroads; post village in Harford County.

Upper Fairmont; post village in Somerset County.

Upper Ferry; village in Wicomico County.

Upper Hunting; creek, a small tributary of Choptank River in Dorchester County.

Upper Marlboro; county seat of Prince George County on the Chesapeake Beach Railway. Population, 447.

Urbana; village in Frederick County.

Vale; post village in Harford County.

Vale; run, a small tributary of Georges Creek in Allegany County.

Valentine; creek, a small tributary of Severn River in Anne Arundel County.

Vale Summit; post village and station in Allegany County on the George's Creek and Cumberland Railroad.

Valley Lee; post village in St. Mary County.

Valliant; post village in Talbot County.

Van Bibber; post village in Harford County on the Baltimore and Ohio Railroad.

Veazey; neck, a strip of land lying between Bohemia River and Cabin John Creek in Cecil County.

Velvet Rock; branch, a small tributary of Susquehanna River in Harford County.

Verona; village in Baltimore County.

Victor; village in Somerset County.

Vienna; post village in Dorchester County on the Baltimore, Chesapeake and Atlantic Railway.

Wades; point in Talbot County, projecting into Eastern Bay.

Wagram; creek, a small tributary of Pocomoke River in Worcester County.

Wakefield; post village in Carroll County on the Western Maryland Railroad.

Walbrook; suburb of Baltimore City within its chartered limits on the Western Maryland Railroad.

Waldorf; post village in Charles County on the Philadelphia, Baltimore and Washington Railroad.

Walker; village in Baltimore County on the Northern Central Railway.

Walkers Switch; post village in Baltimore County.

Walkersville; town in Frederick County on the Northern Central Railway. Population, 359.

Wallace; creek, a small tributary of Honga River in Dorchester County.

Wallman; post village in Garrett County.

Wallville; post village in Calvert County.

Walnut; hill, a summit in Pea Ridge in Garrett County. Elevation, 2,770 feet.

Walnut; point in Anne Arundel County, projecting into Curtis Creek.

Walnut; small mountain ridge in Allegany County lying between Collier and Warrior mountains.

Walnut; village in Wicomico County.

Walston; village in Wicomico County on the Baltimore, Chesapeake and Atlantic Railway.

Walters; post village in Baltimore County.

Wango; village in Wicomico County.

Wann; cove, a small inlet of East Fork of Langford Bay in Kent County.

Ward; village in Somerset County on the New York, Philadelphia and Norfolk Railroad.

Ward Chapel; village in Baltimore County.

Warehouse; creek, a small tributary of Cox Creek in Queen Anne County.

Waring; village in Montgomery County on the Baltimore and Ohio Railroad.

Warntel; run, a small tributary of Savage Run in Garrett County.

Warren; post village in Baltimore County.

Warrior; small mountain ridge in Allegany County.

Warrior; run, a small tributary of North Branch of Potomac River in Allegany County.

Warwick; point, a summit on east bank of Savage River in Garrett County.

Warwick; post village in Cecil County.

Washington; county, situated in the western mountainous portion of the State, bounded on the north by Pennsylvania, east by Blue Ridge Mountains, south and southwest by Potomac River, and west by Allegany County. The surface is an alternation of ridges and valleys, the latter being drained by Antietam, Conococheague, and Israel creeks. The area is 458 square miles, of which more than two-thirds, or 197,948 acres, was under cultivation in 1900. The population for the same year was 45,133. The county seat is Hagerstown. Other towns are Sharpsburg and Williamsport, having populations of 1,030 and 1,472, respectively. The average magnetic declination in the county in 1900 was 4° 30'. The annual rainfall commonly ranges between 45 and 50 inches, and the mean annual temperature between 45° and 50°.

Washington; creek, a small tributary of Patuxent River in St. Mary County.

Washington Grove; post village in Montgomery County on the Baltimore and Ohio Railroad.

Washington Junction; station in Frederick County on the Baltimore and Ohio Railroad.

Waterbury; post village in Anne Arundel County on the Annapolis, Washington and Baltimore Railroad.

Waterhole; cove, a small inlet of Harris Bay in Talbot County.

Waterloo; village in Howard County.

Watersville; post village in Carroll County on the Baltimore and Ohio Railroad.

Waterworks; creek, a small tributary to Chincoteague Bay in Worcester County.

Watkins; point in Somerset County, projecting into Pocomoke River.

Watkins; post village in Montgomery County.

Watts; branch, a small tributary of Potomac River in Montgomery County.

Watts; creek, a small tributary of Choptank River in Caroline County.

Waverly; suburb of Baltimore City within its chartered limits.

Wayside; post village in Charles County.

Wear; point in Somerset County, projecting into Big Annemessex River.

Webster; post village in Harford County.

Weem; creek, a small tributary of Severn River in Anne Arundel County.

Weir; point in Baltimore County, projecting into Bush River.

Weisburg; village in Baltimore County.

Welbourne; post village in Worcester County.

Welcome; post village in Charles County.

Wellhams; post village in Anne Arundel County on the Baltimore and Annapolis Short Line Railroad.

Wellington; post village in Somerset County.

Wellridge; creek, a small tributary to Tangier Sound in Somerset County.

Welsh; point in Cecil County, projecting into Elk River.

Welshman; creek, a small tributary of Patapsco River.

Wenona; post village in Somerset County.

Wesley; post village in Worcester County on the Philadelphia, Baltimore and Washington Railroad.

West; branch, a small tributary of Jones Falls Creek in Baltimore County.

West; branch, a small tributary of Little Elk River in Cecil County.

West; branch, a small tributary of Little Northeast Branch in Cecil County.

West; branch, a small stream heading in Cecil County and flowing through Delaware into Persimmon Run.

West; small branch of Winters Creek in Harford County.

West; creek, a small tributary of Little Annemessex River in Somerset County.

West; river, a tributary to Chesapeake Bay in Anne Arundel County.

West; village in Somerset County.

West Beavercreek; post village in Washington County.

Western; branch, a small tributary of Patuxent River in Prince George County.

Western; group of small marshy islands at mouth of Goose Creek in Somerset County.

Western; run, a small tributary of Beaver Dam Creek in Baltimore County.

Westernport; town in Allegany County on the West Virginia Central and Pittsburg Railroad. Population, 1,008.

Western Run; post village in Baltimore County.

West Falls; village in Carroll County.

West Friendship; post village in Howard County.

West Liberty; village in Baltimore County.

Westminster; county seat of Carroll County on the Western Maryland Railroad. Population, 3,199.

Westover; post village in Somerset County on the New York, Philadelphia and Norfolk Railroad.

Westphalia; post village in Prince George County.

West River; post village in Anne Arundel County.

Westwood; post village in Prince George County.

Wetipquin; post village in Wicomico County.

Weverton; post village in Washington County on the Baltimore and Ohio Railroad.

Whaleysville; post village in Worcester County on the Baltimore, Chesapeake and Atlantic Railway.

Whayland; post village in Wicomico County.

Wheaton; post village in Montgomery County.

Wheel; post village in Harford County.

Whiteburg; post village in Worcester County.

Whiteford; post village in Harford County.

Whitehall; post village in Baltimore County on the Northern Central Railway.

Whitehaven; post village in Wicomico County.

White Knob; mountain in Garrett County.

Whiteleysburg; post village in Caroline County.

Whitemarsh; creek, a small tributary of Rhode River in Anne Arundel County.

Whitemarsh; post village in Baltimore County.

Whitemarsh; run, a small tributary of Horning Run in Baltimore County.

White Meadow; run, a small branch of Cherry Run in Garrett County.

White Neck; creek, a small tributary to St. Catharine Sound in St. Mary County.

Whiteoak; point in Baltimore County, projecting into Bush River.

Whiteoak; run, a small tributary to North Branch of Patapsco River in Carroll County.

Whiteoak; village in Montgomery County on the Philadelphia, Baltimore and Washington Railroad.

Whiteoak Spring; run, a small branch of Muddy Creek in Garrett County.

Whiteplains; post village in Charles County.

White Rock; small island in Patapsco River in Anne Arundel County.

White Rock; run, a small tributary of Youghiogheny River in Garrett County.

Whites Ferry; post village in Montgomery County.

White Sulphur; small branch of Fifteenmile Creek in Allegany County.

Whitneys; landing on Severn River in Anne Arundel County.

Vhiton; post village in Wicomico County.

Whittington; point in Worcester County, projecting into Chincoteague Bay.

Wicomico; county, organized in 1867 from portions of Somerset and Worcester counties, with the following boundaries: north, the south boundary of the State of Delaware; east, Pocomoke River; south, Somerset and Worcester counties, and west, Nanticoke River. The surface is level. The area is 365 square miles, of which more than one-half, or 122,453 acres, was under cultivation in 1900. The county seat is Salisbury, with a population of 4,277 in 1900. The average magnetic declination in the county in 1900 was 5° 15'. The rainfall commonly ranges between 45 and 50 inches, and the mean annual temperature between 55° and 60°.

Wicomico; post village in Charles County.

Wicomico; river, an estuary on the north side of Potomac River in Charles and St. Mary counties, forming the boundary line between the two counties. Two streams, known as Zekiah and Gilbert swamps, flow into it at its head.

Wicomico; river on the east shore of Maryland heading on the south boundary of Delaware and flowing southwest into Tangier Sound, an arm of Chesapeake Bay. Much of its course is bordered by marshes. Near its mouth it forms an estuary.

Widgeon; village in Somerset County.

Wild Cat; small branch of Great Seneca Creek in Montgomery County.

Wild Cat; creek, a small branch of Little Bennetts Creek in Montgomery County.

Wild Cat; point in Cecil County, projecting into Susquehanna River.

Willards; post village in Wicomico County on the Baltimore, Chesapeake and Atlantic Railway.

Williams; point in Somerset County, projecting into Pocomoke River.

Bull. 231—04——6

Williamsburg; post village in Dorchester County.

Williamsport; town in Washington County on the Cumberland Valley and the Western Maryland railroads. Population, 1,472.

Williston; post village in Caroline County.

Willoughby; post village in Queen Anne County on the Queen Anne's Railroad.

Willows; post village in Calvert County.

Wills; creek, a small stream rising in Pennsylvania and flowing into North Branch of Potomac River in Allegany County.

Wills; mountain, a continuation of Knobby Mountain of West Virginia. Elevation, 1,877 feet.

Wilna; post village in Harford County.

Wilson; point in Harford County, projecting into Bush River.

Wilson; point in Baltimore County, projecting into Middle River.

Wilson; point in Kent County, projecting into Chesapeake Bay.

Wilson; wharf on Magothy River in Anne Arundel County.

Wilson Point; wharf on Sassafras River in Kent County.

Wimbledon; post village in Harford County.

Wimms; branch, a small tributary of Horsepen Branch in Prince George County.

Winans; station in Baltimore County on the Philadelphia, Baltimore and Washington Railroad.

Winans; cove, a small inlet of Patapsco River in Baltimore County.

Winchester; creek, a small tributary of Chester River in Queen Anne County.

Winchester; village in Anne Arundel County on the Baltimore and Annapolis Short Line Railroad.

Winding; mountain ridge in Garrett County. Elevation, 2,866 feet.

Windlass; run, a small branch of Bird River in Baltimore County.

Windmill; creek, a small branch of St. Martin River in Worcester County.

Windmill; point in Charles County, projecting into Potomac River.

Windmill; point in Dorchester County, projecting into Honga River.

Windmill; point in St. Mary County, projecting into St. Mary River.

Windsor; creek, a small tributary of Nanticoke River in Wicomico County.

Windyhill; post village in Talbot County.

Winebrenner; run, a small stream rising in Garrett County and flowing into Georges Creek in Allegany County.

Winfield; village in Carroll County.

Wingate; point in Dorchester County, projecting into Honga River.

Wingate; post village in Dorchester County.

Winter; run, a small tributary of Patapsco River in Carroll County.

Winters; run, a small branch of Otter Point Creek in Harford County.

Wire; pond, a small inlet of Isle of Wight Bay in Worcester County.

Witchcoate; point in Baltimore County, projecting into Back River.

Wittman; post village in Talbot County.

Wolf; gap in Big Savage Mountain in Garrett County.

Wolf; rock, a summit in Dans Mountain in Allegany County. Elevation, 2,796 feet.

Wolfden; run, a small tributary of North Branch of Potomac River in Garrett County.

Wolfe Mill; village in Allegany County.

Wolftrap; creek, a small tributary of Manokin River in Somerset County.

Wolsey; creek, a small tributary of Chester River in Queen Anne County.

Wood; small island in Susquehanna River in Harford County.

Woodberry; suburb of Baltimore City within its chartered limits.

Woodbine; post village and station in Carroll County on the Baltimore and Ohio Railroad.

GANNETT.] GAZETTEER OF MARYLAND. **83**

Woodbrook; post village in Baltimore County on the Maryland and Pennsylvania Railroad.

Woodensburg; post village in Baltimore County on the Western Maryland Railroad.

Woodfield; post village in Montgomery County.

Woodland; creek, a small tributary of Miles River in Talbot County.

Woodland; post village in Talbot County.

Woodlawn; village in Cecil County.

Woodmore; post village in Prince George County.

Woods; point in Worcester County, projecting into St. Martin River.

Woodsboro; post village in Frederick County on the Northern Central Railway.

Woodside; post village in Montgomery County on the Baltimore and Ohio Railroad.

Woodstock; post village in Howard County on the Baltimore and Ohio Railroad.

Woodville; village in Frederick County on the Washington, Potomac and Chesapeake Railroad.

Woodwardville; post village in Anne Arundel County.

Woodyard; village in Prince George County.

Woolford; creek, a small tributary of Little Choptank River in Dorchester County.

Woolford; neck, a strip of land lying between Woolford Creek and Madison Bay in Dorchester County.

Woolford; post village in Dorchester County.

Worcester; county, organized in 1742, occupies the extreme southeast corner of the State, and comprises the whole of the Maryland ocean front. It is bounded on the north by Wicomico County and the State of Delaware, east by the ocean, and south by the ocean and Virginia, and west by Pocomoke River. The surface of the county is low and level, in some places rising only 5 feet above the sea. The Atlantic coast is bordered by sand bars separated from the mainland by lagoons known as Assawoman and Sinepuxent bays, having marshy shores. The area is 487 square miles, of which more than a third, or 132,549 acres, was under cultivation in 1900. The population for the same year was 20,865. The county seat is Snow Hill, with a population of 1,576. Other towns are Pocomoke and Berlin, with populations of 2,248 and 1,246, respectively. The average magnetic declination in the county in 1900 was 5° 05′. The rainfall commonly ranges between 45 and 50 inches, and the mean annual temperature, between 45° and 50°.

Worlds End; creek, a small tributary of Charles Creek in Dorchester County.

Worton; creek, a small tributary to Chesapeake Bay in Kent County.

Worton; point in Kent County, projecting into Chesapeake Bay.

Worton; post village in Kent County on the Philadelphia, Baltimore and Washington Railroad.

Wrights; branch, a small tributary of Nanticoke River in Dorchester County.

Wrights; post village in Dorchester County.

Wrights; run, a small tributary of Georges Creek in Allegany County.

Wroten; small, almost entirely marshy island in Honga River in Dorchester County.

Wroths; point in Cecil County, projecting into Elk River.

Wye; landing on Wye River in Talbot County.

Wye; landing on Wye River in Queen Anne County.

Wye Mills; village in Talbot County.

Wye; narrows, a passage connecting Back and Front Wye rivers in Queen Anne County.

Wye; river, a tributary to Eastern Bay in Queen Anne County.

Wynne; post village in St. Mary County.

Yellow; branch, a small tributary of Little Gunpowder Falls in Harford County.

Yellow Springs; village in Frederick County.

Yeoho; village in Baltimore County.

Youghiogheny; river, the largest branch of the Monongahela River, rises in the northern part of West Virginia, flows nearly north across the western part of Maryland and joins the Monongahela River a few miles above its mouth at Pittsburg.

Youngs Switch; village in Charles County.

Zekiah; swamp, a small marshy stream flowing into Wicomico River in Charles County.

Zion; village in Cecil County.

Zippy; creek, a small branch of St. Martin River in Worcester County.

O

58TH CONGRESS, } HOUSE OF REPRESENTATIVES. { DOCUMENT
2d Session. } { No. 725.

Bulletin No. 230   Series F, Geography, 38

DEPARTMENT OF THE INTERIOR

UNITED STATES GEOLOGICAL SURVEY

CHARLES D. WALCOTT, DIRECTOR

A

GAZETTEER OF DELAWARE

BY

HENRY GANNETT

WASHINGTON

GOVERNMENT PRINTING OFFICE

1904

LETTER OF TRANSMITTAL.

DEPARTMENT OF THE INTERIOR,
UNITED STATES GEOLOGICAL SURVEY,
Washington, D. C., March 9, 1904.

SIR: I have the honor to transmit herewith, for publication as a bulletin, a gazetteer of Delaware.

Very respectfully,

HENRY GANNETT,
Geographer.

Hon. CHARLES D. WALCOTT,
Director United States Geological Survey.

3

A GAZETTEER OF DELAWARE.

By HENRY GANNETT.

GENERAL DESCRIPTION OF THE STATE.

Delaware is one of the Middle States, and borders upon Delaware Bay and the Atlantic Ocean between latitudes 38° 30' and 39° 45', and between longitudes 75° 00' and 75° 50'. The east boundary of the State is Delaware Bay and the Atlantic Ocean. The south boundary is a line beginning at Cape Henlopen—as the name was originally applied—in latitude 38° 27', and running due west 34 miles 309 perches. The west boundary is a straight line, commencing at the westernmost point on the southern boundary and running northward 81 miles 78 chains and 30 links until it touches and makes a tangent to the western periphery of a circle with a radius of 12 statute miles from the center of the town of Newcastle. The north boundary is the periphery of this circle as far as Delaware River.

Delaware was first settled by the Dutch in 1629. In 1638 the Swedes made a settlement and held the colony until 1655, when it was surrendered to the Dutch. In 1664 this region, with the other Dutch possessions, was acquired by the Duke of York. In 1682 this territory passed from the Duke of York to William Penn by deed, and was held by him until 1701, when he granted it a charter enabling its people to set up a separate government. Delaware is one of the thirteen original States, and was the first to adopt the Constitution, taking this step December 7, 1787.

The population of the State in 1900 was 184,735. The following table gives the population at each census since 1790:

Population of Delaware at each census since 1790.

1790	59,096
1800	64,273
1810	72,674
1820	72,749
1830	76,748
1840	78,085
1850	91,532
1860	112,216
1870	125,015
1880	146,608
1890	168,493
1900	184,735

The density of population in 1900 was 94.3 inhabitants to a square mile. The chief city is Wilmington, with a population of 76,508 in 1900; the capital is Dover, with a population of 3,329 in 1900. The urban population in 1900 amounted to about 54 per cent. As to sexes, the population is divided in the proportion of 51 males to 49 females. The State contains 30,697 negroes, five-sixths of the population being white, while one-sixth is colored. The proportion of foreign born is small, only 7.5 per cent of the inhabitants being foreign born, to 92.5 per cent native born.

Of the total population 10 years of age and over, 12 per cent were unable to read and write. This illiteracy was, however, found mainly among negroes. The illiterate element of the whites consisted of only 7 per cent of the whole number, while that of the negroes constituted 38 per cent. Of the total population over 15 years of age, 36 per cent were single, 55 per cent married, 8 per cent widowed, and 0.2 per cent divorced.

Of the entire number of inhabitants over 10 years of age, almost exactly one-half were engaged in gainful occupations. Of the males not less than 81 per cent were wage-earners, and of the females 18 per cent. The wage-earners were distributed in the following proportions among the five grand divisions of occupations:

Proportions of wage-earners in Delaware in 1900.

	Per cent.
Agriculture	26
Professions	4
Domestic and personal service	23
Trade and transportation	16
Manufacturing	31

In 1900 there were 9,687 farms in the State, of which more than nine-tenths were operated by white farmers. Of the entire number of farms, just one-half were operated by their owners and the other half by tenants. The area of land in farms was 1,066,228 acres, of which 754,010 acres were improved. The average size of the farms was 110 acres, which is considerably less than the average of the country. The improved area amounted to 71 per cent of the total farm area and 60 per cent of the total area of the State. The value of all the farm property was $40,697,654, of which $34,436,040 consisted of land and buildings, $2,150,560 of farm implements and machinery, and $4,111,054 of live stock. The farm products were valued at $9,290,777. The average value per farm of all farm property was $4,201, and the value of products per farm was $959. The following table gives the number of animals upon farms:

Animals on farms in Delaware in 1900.

Meat cattle 54, 180
Horses 29, 722
Mules 4, 745
Sheep 11, 765
Swine ....\.. 46, 732

The following table gives the amounts of farm products in 1900:

Farm products of Delaware in 1900.

Corn ....bushels.. 4, 736, 580
Wheat ....do.... 1, 870, 570
Oats ....do....   131, 960
Hay and other forage...tons..... 128, 193
Potatoes...bushels..   414, 610
Sweet potatoes...do....   222, 165
Dairy products.. $1, 092, 807

The total number of manufacturing establishments in the State in 1900 was 1,417, with a total capital of $41,203,239 and 22,303 employees. The wages paid annually amounted to $9,259,661, the value of materials to $26,652,601, and the value of products to $45,387,630.

GAZETTEER.

Angola; post village in Sussex County near the coast.

Appoquinimink; small creek in Newcastle County, which flows eastward into Delaware Bay.

Argo; post village in Sussex County.

Armstrong; railroad station in Newcastle County on Philadelphia, Baltimore and Washington Railroad.

Ashland; post village in Newcastle County on the Baltimore and Ohio Railroad.

Bacons; post village in Sussex County.

Bayard; post village in Sussex County.

Bayville; post village in Sussex County.

Bear; post village in Newcastle County on the Philadelphia, Baltimore and Washington Railroad.

Beavervalley; small town in Newcastle County, near Wilmington.

Bellevue; post village in Newcastle County on Delaware River and on the Philadelphia, Baltimore and Washington Railroad.

Berrytown; village in Kent County.

Bethel; post village in Sussex County.

Bingham; station in Kent County on the Baltimore and Delaware Bay Railroad.

Blackbird; creek, a small left-hand branch of Duck Creek, a tributary of Delaware River.

Blackbird; post village in Newcastle County on the Philadelphia, Baltimore and Washington Railroad.

Blackistone; village in Kent County.

Blackwater; village in Sussex County.

Blades; post village in Sussex County.

Blanchard; post village in Sussex County on the Queen Anne's Railroad.

Bombay; hook, a point in Kent County projecting into Delaware Bay.

Bombay Hook; island in Kent County; it has Delaware Bay on the east, and is divided from the mainland by Duck Creek.

Bowers; village in Kent County.

Brandywine; post village in Newcastle County in the northernmost hundred in the State.

Brenford; post village in Kent County, 8 miles north of Dover, on the Philadelphia, Baltimore and Washington Railroad.

Bridgeville; town in Sussex County, near Nanticoke River, on the Philadelphia, Baltimore and Washington Railroad. Population, 613.

Broad; creek, a small left-hand tributary to Nanticoke River.

Broad Kiln; small creek in Sussex County flowing into Delaware Bay.

Brownsville; village in Kent County.

Bunting; post village in Sussex County.

Camden; town in Kent County, near Dover. Population, 536.

8

Cannon; post village in Sussex County on the Philadelphia, Baltimore and Washington Railroad.

Canterbury; village in Kent County near Dover.

Carpenter; post village in Newcastle County on the Baltimore and Ohio Railroad.

Carrcroft; post village in Newcastle County on the Baltimore and Ohio Railroad.

Cedar; creek, rising in Sussex County and flowing east into Delaware Bay.

Cedar; island at entrance of Rehoboth Bay.

Cedar Creek; village in Sussex County.

Centerville; post village in Newcastle County near Wilmington.

Chambersville; village in Newcastle County.

Chestnut; hill in Newcastle County. Elevation, 280 feet.

Cheswold; town in Kent County on the Philadelphia, Baltimore and Washington Railroad. Population, 201.

Choate; post village in Newcastle County.

Christiana; creek, formed by Red Clay and White Clay creeks, which unite in Newcastle County. It runs northeastward and enters Delaware River about 2 miles below Wilmington.

Christiana; post village in Newcastle County.

Clark; point in Kent County projecting into Delaware Bay.

Clarksville; post village in Sussex County.

Claymont; post village in Newcastle County on Delaware River and on the Philadelphia, Baltimore and Washington Railroad.

Clayton; town in Kent County on Duck Creek on the Philadelphia, Baltimore and Washington Railroad. Population, 819.

Columbia; post village in Sussex County.

Concord; town in Newcastle County on the Baltimore and Ohio Railroad.

Concord; post village in Sussex County near Nanticoke River.

Coochs Bridge; post village near Delaware City in Newcastle County, known as Cooch, on the Philadelphia, Baltimore and Washington Railroad.

Coolspring; post village in Sussex County on the Philadelphia, Baltimore and Washington Railroad.

Coopers Corners; village in Kent County.

Corbit; station in Newcastle County on the Philadelphia, Baltimore and Washington Railroad.

Cowgill; village in Kent County.

Cowmarsh; ditch, branch of Chotank River in Kent County.

Cranberry; branch, a tributary to Delaware Bay in Kent County.

Dagsboro; town in Sussex County on the Philadelphia, Baltimore and Washington Railroad. Population, 190.

Deakyneville; village in Newcastle County.

Deep; creek, a head fork of Nanticoke River.in Sussex County.

Deepwater; marshy point in Kent County projecting into Delaware Bay.

Delaney; post village in Newcastle County on the Philadelphia, Baltimore and Washington Railroad.

Delaware; bay, an inlet of the sea, or an estuary, through which Delaware River enters the Atlantic Ocean. The entrance of the bay, which is between Cape May and Cape Henlopen, is about 13 miles wide and its length is about 55 miles.

Delaware; river, formed by two branches sometimes called the Coquago and the Popacton, which rise in New York near the northeastern border of Delaware County and unite at Hancock in the same county. From this point it runs southeastward, forming the boundary between New York and Pennsylvania, until it reaches Port Jervis and touches the northern extremity of New Jersey. Here Kittatinny Mountain causes it to change its course and run southwestward along the base of that ridge to the Delaware Water Gap near Stroudsburg. About

40 miles below Philadelphia it expands into an estuary called Delaware Bay. This river forms the entire boundary between New Jersey and Pennsylvania. The length of the main stream is estimated to be about 280 miles; the mean discharge, 18,619 second-feet at Lambertville, N. J.; navigable to Trenton. Drainage area, 12,012 square miles.

Delaware City; city in Newcastle County on the Philadelphia, Baltimore and Washington Railroad, situated on Delaware River where it merges into Delaware Bay, about 12 miles southwest of Wilmington. Population, 1,132.

Delmar; town in Sussex County on the New York, Philadelphia and Norfolk and the Philadelphia, Baltimore and Washington railroads. Population, 444.

Dover; town and county seat of Kent County, situated on St. Jones Creek and on the Philadelphia, Baltimore and Washington Railroad, about 6 miles west of Delaware Bay.

Downs Chapel; post village in Kent County.

Drawbridge; post village in Sussex County near Delaware Bay.

Drawyer; creek, a small tributary to Delaware Bay in Newcastle County.

Duck; creek, forms the boundary between Kent and Newcastle counties and empties into Delaware Bay.

Dupont; station in Kent County on the Philadelphia, Baltimore and Washington Railroad.

Dyke; branch, a tributary to Delaware Bay in Kent County.

Eagles Nest; landing on Smyrna River on boundary between Newcastle and Kent counties.

Edgemoor; post village in Newcastle County on the Philadelphia, Baltimore and Washington Railroad about 3 miles from Wilmington.

Edwardsville; village in Kent County.

Ellendale; post village in Sussex County on the Philadelphia, Baltimore and Washington and the Queen Anne's railroads.

Elsmere; post village in Newcastle County on the Baltimore and Ohio Railroad.

Fairmont; post village in Sussex County.

Farmington; post village in Kent County on the Philadelphia, Baltimore and Washington Railroad.

Farnhurst; post village in Newcastle County on the Philadelphia, Baltimore and Washington Railroad.

Faulkland; post village in Newcastle County on the Baltimore and Ohio Railroad.

Felton; town and post village in Kent County on the Philadelphia, Baltimore and Washington Railroad.

Fennimore; landing on Appoquinimink Creek in Newcastle County.

Fieldsboro; village in Newcastle County.

Forest; post village in Newcastle County.

Frankford; town in Sussex County on the Philadelphia, Baltimore and Washington Railroad.

Frederica; town in Kent County on Murderkill Creek. Population, 706.

Georgetown; town and county seat of Sussex County on the Philadelphia, Baltimore and Washington Railroad. Population, 1,658.

Glasgow; post village in Newcastle County on the Philadelphia, Baltimore and Washington Railroad.

Goose; marshy point in Kent County projecting into Delaware Bay.

Granogue; post village in Newcastle County on the Philadelphia and Reading Railway.

Gravelly Branch; creek, a head branch of Nanticoke River in Sussex County.

Green; branch of Smyrna River in Kent County.

Green Spring; village in Newcastle County on the Philadelphia, Baltimore and Washington Railroad.

Greenville; post village in Newcastle County on the Philadelphia and Reading Railway.

Greenwood; post village in Sussex County on the Philadelphia, Baltimore and Washington and the Queen Anne's railroads.

Grubbs; post village in Newcastle County.

Gumboro; post village in Sussex County.

Guyencourt; post village in Newcastle County on the Philadelphia and Reading Railway.

Hangmans Run; a small tributary to Delaware Bay in Newcastle County.

Harbeson; post village in Sussex County, known as Broadkill, on the Philadelphia, Baltimore and Washington Railroad.

Harrington; town in Kent County on the Philadelphia, Baltimore and Washington Railroad. Population, 1,242.

Hartly; post village in Kent County on the Philadelphia, Baltimore and Washington Railroad.

Hazlettville; village in Kent County.

Henlopen; cape on the eastern coast of Delaware at the entrance of Delaware Bay.

Henry Clay Factory; post village in Newcastle County.

Herring; small creek rising in Sussex County and flowing east into Rehoboth Bay.

Hickman; post village in Kent County on the Queen Anne's Railroad.

Hockessin; post village in Newcastle County.

Hollandville; village in Kent County.

Hollyoak; post village in Newcastle County on the Philadelphia, Baltimore and Washington Railroad.

Hollyville; post village in Sussex County.

Houston Station; post village in Kent County on the Philadelphia, Baltimore and Washington Railroad.

Indian; river of Sussex County flowing eastward into the Atlantic Ocean.

Iron; hill in Newcastle County. Altitude, 340 feet.

Isaac; branch of St. Jones Creek in Kent County.

Keeney; station in Newcastle County on Philadelphia, Baltimore and Washington Railroad.

Kelleys; small island in Delaware Bay near the coast.

Kent; county, situated in the central part of the State, bounded on the east by Delaware Bay and drained by Choptank River and Duck and Mispillion creeks. The surface is extensively covered with forests. The soil is mostly fertile; area, 615 square miles; population, 32,762; white, 25,017; negro, 7,738; foreign born, 626; county seat, Dover. The mean magnetic declination in 1900 was 6° 30′; the mean annual rainfall about 45 inches, and the mean annual temperature, about 50°. The county is traversed by the Philadelphia, Baltimore and Washington Railroad.

Kenton; town and post village in Kent County on the Philadelphia, Baltimore and Washington Railroad. Population, 192.

Kirkwood; post village in Newcastle County on the Philadelphia, Baltimore and Washington Railroad.

Knowles; post village in Sussex County.

Lambs; village in Sussex County.

Laurel; town in Sussex County on the Philadelphia, Baltimore and Washington Railroad. Population, 825.

Lebanon; village in Kent County.

Leipsic; town in Kent County. Population, 305.

Lewes; creek, a very small branch rising in Sussex County and flowing north into Delaware Bay.

Lewes; town in Sussex County on the Philadelphia, Baltimore and Washington and the Queen Anne's railroads. Population, 2,259.

Lincoln; post village in Sussex County on the Philadelphia, Baltimore and Washington Railroad.

Lisbon; point in Newcastle County projecting into Delaware Bay.

Little; creek rising in Kent County and emptying into Delaware Bay.

Little Bombay Hook; small marshy island in Delaware Bay in Kent County near mouth of Delaware River.

Littlecreek; town in Kent County. Population, 259.

Little Duck; creek, a tributary to Delaware Bay in Kent County.

Love; creek, rises in Sussex County and empties into Rehoboth Bay.

Lowes Crossroads; village in Sussex County.

McClellandsville; post village in Newcastle County.

McDonough; post village in Newcastle County.

Magnolia; town in Kent County. Population, 208.

Marshallton; post village in Newcastle County on the Baltimore and Ohio Railroad.

Marydel; village on boundary line between Delaware and Maryland on the Philadelphia, Baltimore and Washington Railroad.

Masten; village in Kent County.

Middle; creek, a small right-hand tributary to Indian River in Sussex County.

Middleford; post village in Sussex County on Nanticoke River.

Middletown; town in Newcastle County on the Philadelphia, Baltimore and Washington Railroad. Population, 1,567.

Midway; post village in Sussex County.

Milford; town in Kent County on the Philadelphia, Baltimore and Washington Railroad. Population, 2,500.

Mill; creek, a branch of Smyrna River in Kent County.

Millsboro; town in Sussex County on the Philadelphia, Baltimore and Washington Railroad. Population, 391.

Millville; post village in Sussex County.

Milton; town in Sussex County on the Queen Anne's Railroad. Population, 948.

Mispillion; small creek forming the boundary between Sussex and Kent counties and flowing into Delaware Bay.

Mission; village in Sussex County.

Montchanin; post village in Newcastle County on the Philadelphia and Reading Railway.

Morris; branch of Smyrna River in Newcastle County.

Mount Cuba; post village in Newcastle County on the Baltimore and Ohio Railroad.

Mount Pleasant; post village in Newcastle County on the Philadelphia, Baltimore and Washington Railroad.

Mudstone; branch of St. Jones Creek in Kent County.

Murder Hill; small creek rising in Kent County and flowing into Delaware Bay.

Nanticoke; river, rises in Sussex County and runs southwestward into Maryland, where it forms the boundary between the counties of Dorchester and Wicomico, and enters Chesapeake Bay at the western extremity of the latter county. Length, 75 miles.

Nassau; post village in Sussex County on the Philadelphia, Baltimore and Washington Railroad.

Newark; town in Newcastle County on the Baltimore and Ohio and the Philadelphia, Baltimore and Washington railroads. Population, 1,213.

Newcastle; city in Newcastle County on the Philadelphia, Baltimore and Washington Railroad, situated on the Delaware River. Population, 3,380.

Newcastle; county, the most northern of the State, bordering on Pennsylvania. It is bounded on the east by Delaware River and Bay and is drained by Brandywine, Christiana, Red Clay, and Duck creeks. The surface is undulating; the soil is fertile. Area, 434 square miles. Population, 109,697; white, 93,454; negro, 16,197; foreign born, 12,916. County seat, Wilmington. The mean magnetic declination in 1900 was 6° 05′; the mean annual rainfall, 45 inches; and the temperature, 50° 00′. The county is traversed by the Baltimore and Ohio, the Philadelphia and Reading, and the Philadelphia, Baltimore and Washington railroads.

Newport; town in Newcastle County on Christiana Creek and on the Philadelphia, Baltimore and Washington Railroad.

Northwest; branch of Smyrna River in Newcastle County.

Noxontown; pond on headwaters of Appoquinimink Creek in Newcastle County.

Oakel; village in Sussex County.

Oakgrove; post village in Sussex County on the Philadelphia, Baltimore and Washington Railroad.

Oakley; post village in Sussex County on the Queen Anne's Railroad.

Oceanview; post village in Sussex County near the ocean.

Odessa; town in Newcastle County on Appoquinimink Creek.

Omar; post village in Sussex County.

Overbrook; post village in Sussex County on the Queen Anne's Railroad.

Owens; post village in Sussex County on the Queen Anne's Railroad.

Pearson; village in Kent County.

Pepper; small creek emptying into Indian Bay in Sussex County.

Pepper; village in Sussex County.

Petersburg; village in Kent County.

Porter; post village in Newcastle County on the Philadelphia, Baltimore and Washington Railroad.

Port Mahon; landing on shore of Delaware Bay in Kent County.

Port Penn; town in Newcastle County. Population, 304.

Price Corners; village in Newcastle County.

Prime Hook; creek, rising in Sussex County and emptying into Delaware Bay.

Providence; creek, a branch of Smyrna River in Newcastle County.

Puncheon; branch of St. Jones Creek in Kent County.

Ralph; post village in Sussex County.

Redden; post village in Sussex County on Philadelphia, Baltimore and Washington Railroad.

Red Lion; creek, a very small right-hand branch of Delaware River in Newcastle County.

Redlion; post village in Newcastle County.

Reedy; island at head of Delaware Bay.

Rehoboth; bay, on the coast about 10 miles south of Cape Henlopen, separated from the Atlantic Ocean by a narrow peninsula. It connects on the south with Indian River Bay.

Rehoboth; town in Sussex County on the Philadelphia, Baltimore and Washington and the Queen Anne's railroads. Population, 198.

Reybold; station in Newcastle County on the Philadelphia, Baltimore and Washington Railroad.

Risingsun; village in Kent County.

Robbins; post village in Sussex County on the Philadelphia, Baltimore and Washington Railroad.

Robinsonville; post village in Sussex County.

Rockland; post village in Newcastle County on Brandywine Creek.

Roxana; post village in Sussex County.

St. Georges; town in Newcastle County. Population, 325.

St. Johns Branch; river, one of the small head branches of Nanticoke River.

St. Jones; creek, a small right-hand tributary to Delaware Bay in Kent County.

Sandtown; village in Kent County.

Sandy; point in Kent County projecting into Delaware Bay.

Scotts; village in Sussex County.

Seaford; town in Sussex County on the Philadelphia, Baltimore and Washington Railroad. Population, 1,724.

Selbyville; post village in Sussex County on the Philadelphia, Baltimore and Washington Railroad.

Seven Hickories; village in Kent County.

Sewell; branch of Chester River in Kent County.

Sheals Branch; small head branch of Indian River, rising in Sussex County.

Shortly; village in Sussex County.

Shorts; landing on Smyrna River on boundary between Newcastle and Kent counties.

Slaughter; village in Kent County on the Philadelphia, Baltimore and Washington Railroad.

Silver Run; small stream in Newcastle county tributary to Delaware Bay.

Smith; post village in Sussex County.

Smyrna; river, tributary to Delaware Bay on boundary between Newcastle and Kent counties.

Smyrna; town in Kent County on the Philadelphia, Baltimore and Washington Railroad. Population, 2,168.

Southwood; station in Newcastle County on the Baltimore and Ohio Railroad.

Spring; creek, a tributary to Delaware Bay in Kent County.

Stanton; post village in Newcastle County, near Christiana Creek, on the Philadelphia, Baltimore and Washington and the Baltimore and Ohio railroads.

Stateroad; post village in Newcastle County on the Philadelphia, Baltimore and Washington Railroad.

Stockley; post village in Sussex County on the Philadelphia, Baltimore and Washington Railroad.

Summit Bridge; post village in Newcastle County on the Chesapeake and Delaware Canal.

Sussex; southernmost county, bordering on Maryland. It is bounded on the east by Delaware Bay and the Atlantic Ocean, and is drained by Nanticoke and Indian rivers and by Mispillion and other creeks. The surface is nearly level, and a large part of it is covered with forests. The soil is mostly fertile; area, 911 square miles. Population, 42,276; white, 35,504; negro, 6,762; foreign born, 268. County seat, Georgetown. The mean magnetic declination in 1900 was 5° 45′; the mean annual rainfall, 45 inches; and the temperature 50°. The county is traversed by the Philadelphia, Baltimore and Washington and the Queen Anne's railroads.

Sycamore; post village in Sussex County.

Talleyville; post village in Newcastle County.

Tanners Branch; river, a small left-hand tributary to Choptank River, rising in Kent County.

Taylors Bridge; post village in Newcastle County.

Thomas Corners; village in Newcastle County.

Thompson; post village in Newcastle County on the Pennsylvania Railroad.

Thompsonville; village in Kent County.

Thoroughfare; neck of land lying between Cedar Swamp and Smyrna River in Newcastle County.

Tidbury; creek, a branch of St. Jones Creek in Kent County.

Townsend; town in Newcastle County on the Philadelphia, Baltimore and Washington Railroad. Population, 399.

Trinity; post village in Sussex County.

Union; village in Newcastle County.

Vance; neck of land lying between Silver River and Drawyer Creek in Newcastle County.

Vandyke; village in Newcastle County on the Philadelphia, Baltimore and Washington Railroad.

Viola; post village in Kent County on the Philadelphia, Baltimore and Washington Railroad.

Walker; village in Newcastle County.

Waples; post village in Sussex County.

Ward; village in Sussex County.

Warwick; post village in Sussex County.

Westville; village in Kent County.

Whitesboro; post village in Sussex County on the Queen Anne's Railroad.

Whitesville; post village in Sussex County.

Wildcat; branch, a tributary to Choptank River in Kent County.

Williamsville; post village in Sussex County.

Willowgrove; village in Kent County.

Wilmington; city and county seat of Newcastle County. Population, 76,508. It is the port of entry, situated on the Delaware River and on the Brandywine and Christiana creeks which unite one-half mile from the river. It is on the Philadelphia, Baltimore and Washington, the Philadelphia and Reading, and the Baltimore and Ohio railroads.

Winterthur; post village in Newcastle County on the Philadelphia and Reading Railway.

Wooddale; post village in Newcastle County on the Baltimore and Ohio Railroad.

Woodland; post village in Sussex County.

Woodside; post village in Kent County on the Philadelphia, Baltimore and Washington Railroad.

Wyoming; town in Kent County on the Philadelphia, Baltimore and Washington Railroad. Population, 450.

Yorklyn; post village in Newcastle County on the Baltimore and Ohio.

O